Seat with a View

Inside the 1996 U.S. Olympic Men's Crew

Steven C. Segaloff

Writers Club Press

San Jose New York Lincoln Shanghai

Seat with a View
Inside the 1996 U.S. Olympic Men's Crew

Published by Writers Club Press
an imprint of iUniverse.com, Inc.

For information address:
iUniverse.com, Inc.
620 North 48th Street
Suite 201
Lincoln, NE 68504-3467
www.iuniverse.com

ISBN: 0-595-09942-4

Printed in the United States of America

Dedication

Throughout my life two groups of people have provided invaluable support–first my friends and family, and second my teammates and coaches. You have all encouraged me to be the best that I can be and always let me know that I was not quite there. This book is for you.

Contents

Foreword

The Coxswain
By Mike Spracklen

He's on his own t'ween coach and crew,
Eight strong men in a shell.
Motivating them while turning the screw.
Applauding when the rowing goes well.

Sometimes there to take the lead,
He's sometimes their spokesman too.
Doing all he can to help them succeed,
There's no limit to what he will do.

He scrubs the oars and cleans the boat,
And the tracks of every seat.
He'll gather up a shirt or coat,
And the shoes from off their feet.

Ready and able as everyone knows,
He does each task with vigour.
Spanner ready where ever he goes.
To fix or adjust a rigger.

Through wind and rain he doesn't wane,
Through freezing ice and torturous sun.
He sits it through ignoring pain.
Committed 'till the job is done.

Willing to help and eager to please
He tends their every whim.
He turns t'other cheek whenever they tease,
And just smiles when they laugh at him.

He may be weak with muscles small,
His diet may not be smart.
Although he's slim and not very tall
He's zealous and big at heart.

He has nerves of steel before a race
When opponents stand big and tall,
He overcomes fear with well controlled grace.
And keeps his crew on the ball.

The starter stands with flag in hand.
His oarsmen ready to row.
Poised and ready at his command.
Nervous but set to go.

With watch afoot and strings to hand,
He'll keep his crew on course,
Changing pace at his command,
He drives them at full force.

He takes the blame when they lose a race.
And even when they win.
Their gratitude is shown with grace,
Head first they throw him in.

But with head up high he makes no slip,
Despite what they do to him.
He always keeps a stiff upper lip.
And takes it all on the chin.

Even when a race is lost.
And pages bad unfold.
Remember what good coxswains cost.
They are worth their weight in GOLD.

Preface

Ninety five percent of the books that come from American Olympians are autobiographies detailing their stories of personal success and achievement. The mega-stars produced by an Olympics–for example, Dan Jansen, Bruce Jenner, Michael Johnson, and Kerri Strug–discuss their lives and show us their paths to the top of the podium. I often dreamed about writing that kind of book. But my Olympic experience was far different.

During my four seasons as a member of the U.S. National Rowing Team, which culminated at the 1996 Summer Olympics, I endeavored to create such a book. I took copious notes on the daily goings on of an elite athlete in international competition in the hopes of creating that type of work.

My four-year tenure as an elite athlete brought many successes–gold medals at major competitions, world travel, and the enviable life of a professional athlete. When our squad marched into the Olympic stadium in 1996 it looked like my dream could become a reality. We may not have been favorites in Atlanta, but by all accounts we were in the thick of the medal hunt.

After four years of preparation for July 28, 1996, the unthinkable happened. We finished fifth. We left Atlanta empty-handed thanks to a very sub-par performance.

This book describes the challenge of striving for a championship; the depression that follows from a defeat; and finally lessons for rebounding from failure. One of my coach's favorite sayings was, "It is the true champion who can lose and then get up to fight again another day." Today I am striving to be that true champion.

Introduction

I am twenty-nine years old, 5'4" and 125 pounds. I am the biggest person in my family in three generations. I was always the smallest in my class, but I was crazy about sports. For as long as I can remember I wanted to be a professional athlete. A little thing like height was not going to stand in my way.

While growing up, my favorite sports were the most popular ones–football, basketball, and baseball. Who cared about rowing? It was never on television. My dreams were big. I wanted to play in big stadiums and become a superstar. Why bother with a sport as unknown as rowing? Even worse, who would want to be a coxswain? What does a coxswain do? It looks like you just sit and yell. Early in life I told my father explicitly, "Coxing is for wimps."

Around my thirteenth birthday I made an unusual request. I wanted to see a doctor about my size, or lack thereof. I pleaded with my parents to take me to a specialist who would measure my wrist in an x-ray. According to a specific formula, the doctor could accurately predict my eventual height. I wanted to know if nature had cursed me forever. My parents caved in and took me to an endocrinologist.

I clearly remember coming home from the hospital that day. The results were not good. Nothing was wrong with me, but the doctor told me I might reach 5'6" if I was lucky. I locked myself in my room and piled up every piece of sports gear or memorabilia for the trash. It was all a waste, I thought. Any hope I had to be an athlete was over. 5'6" was simply too short.

Soon after the wrist measurement ordeal, I watched the 1984 Olympic Trials in Princeton, New Jersey. The rowing trials finals for the 1984 Summer Olympic Games was the first time I remember seeing my father cry. After a successful career in college and club rowing, my Dad still yearned to be an Olympian. At the improbable age of forty-one, he had taken a leave of absence from his law firm, left his family for the summer, and pursued his dream.

After a summer of training, the coaches at the national team camp switched him from one boat into a new crew expected to be very fast. In a cruel twist of fate, the original boat performed magnificently. It went on to represent the U.S. in Los Angeles and won a bronze medal. Meanwhile, my father was inconsolable after the trials. He had come so close, but just missed the last step. That same moment inspired me as a thirteen year-old kid to chase the same dream.

Three Olympiads later I realized my own dream and my father's when I marched into the Olympic Stadium in Atlanta as a member of the 1996 U.S. Olympic Team. It was one of the happiest days of my life. I think my father cried that day, too.

In my freshmen year of high school I started coxing for the first time. My first rowing experience was as a coxswain for the New Haven Rowing Club. My high school did not offer rowing as a sport, and the rowing club was the easiest outlet available. The majority of the oarsmen were masters, meaning that they were aged thirty and above. Most of my crews were comprised of successful middle-aged men who had rowed in college and now spent their early mornings reliving the glory days.

My first launch ride was auspicious. It was the late fall and the temperature was dropping on the Housatonic River in Connecticut. I left our house that morning and my father warned me to dress warmly because it would be very cold. I was a thirteen-year-old know-it-all. How cold could it get? I'll be fine.

The coach and launch driver that day was Dave Vogel, the Yale Lightweight Crew Coach. I jumped into the motorboat and prepared to watch the sport of rowing up-close for the first time. "Are you sure you're going to be warm enough?" Dave asked.

"No problem. I'm fine." I replied.

Ten minutes into our ride I was freezing cold. The brisk air, combined with chilling winds, made the launch an iceboat. I had to take evasive action before my face froze off. Pretty soon I was not paying any attention to the rowing, but rather doing all that I could to regain any sense of feeling in my body. Within half an hour on the water I had crouched below the decks of the tiny boat in a hidden corner to shield myself from the savage winds. This position was far warmer but it also completely blocked any view of the rowing. Great sport.

In time, the New Haven Rowing Club became a far more enjoyable experience. I stopped riding in launches and started steering boats. In one sense, I missed out on the camaraderie of a high school rowing team. Instead of enjoying the typical pranks of teenagers, I spent my time with doctors, lawyers, and professionals from the greater New Haven area. I had to grow up fast. The environment forced me to develop a strong presence in a boat. My responsibility was to organize, and often order, eight men who averaged thirty years older than me. Once I had developed the temerity to scream at those types of teammates I would learn to never be afraid of saying anything to anybody.

Often, though, I helped out with another local program that allowed me to act my age. Yale University's crew was one of the finest in the country and they rowed out of the same boathouse. Through my father's connections with the Yale coaches I arranged to help out with occasional practices. Yale fielded numerous teams, and someone could always use a spare coxswain—men, women, lightweights, heavyweights, freshman, or whatever. When called upon to cox with Yale, I was inevitably put in the worst possible boat, for example, a seven-man crew where two people rowed for the first time. For any other coxswain it would have been a horrible afternoon. But for me those opportunities were my chances to bask in the glorious presence of college heroes.

On two occasions I was invited to try out for the U.S. Junior National Rowing Team. The Junior National Team was chosen from the best high school rowers in the country who represent the country in the Junior World Championships each summer. As a high school rower or coxswain, there is no greater honor than the Junior National Team.

Both times I was rapidly cut from selection camp. My first try I doubt I had time to unpack my bags. I was horribly prepared for either situation. The selection camps were filled with high school athletes who regularly competed against each other throughout the year. I was in the awkward position of coxing for a master's crew. Choosing a coxswain at that age can often become a popularity contest. Since I did not know any high school rowers I never had a chance. I could not relate to the athletes at all and was quickly dismissed. I was crushed emotionally, but not dissuaded from hoping that I could break through someday.

The best thing that came out of my junior camp experience was a friendship. In 1987, I met a rower named Tom Murray from Buffalo, New York. Tom did not know many other rowers and we became fast friends at the camp in Quantico, Virginia. Tom was an extraordinarily powerful rower. While I was sent home in a few days, Tom fought his way into the bow seat of the first American junior eight ever to win a world championship. Little did I realize how integral our friendship would be in my rowing career, or our lives for that matter. In January 1999, Tom served as best man in my wedding.

Tom was a year ahead of me and he headed to Cornell University in the fall. I returned to New Haven for my senior in high school. Cornell's academic reputation spoke for itself. My respect for Tom helped draw me to Cornell and I applied for early decision. I was accepted a few months later and went to Ithaca, New York within the year.

Early in my college experience I was given a nickname that I still haven't shaken. While pledging the fraternity Psi U, also known as Psi Crew, the older brothers named me "Scrappy Doo" after the cartoon character. (Incidentally, my fraternity brother from the same house thirty years earlier is Bill Stowe, stroke of the 1964 U.S. Olympic gold medal eight.) On television, Scrappy is a feisty puppy who is always ready to mix it up with the monsters that face Scooby and his gang. In reality, Scrappy is a loud, annoying, and sometimes obnoxious character. I worked to live up to every aspect of that personality. To this day I am called Scrappy more than my real name. Even my parents use the nickname now and then.

My four years on the Cornell heavyweight rowing team fueled my competitive appetite. I joined a team with a psychology much like my own—aggressive, enthusiastic and of unproven talent. Cornell has one of the proudest rowing traditions in the country. But when I arrived in Ithaca, the squad had endured a significant dry-spell. This bleak recent history was only more motivation for my teammates and I to return Cornell to the elite of the collegiate scene.

The men I rowed with at Cornell were a special group of guys. They were not the biggest, strongest or most technically efficient, but they had enormous heart. Cornell had recruited sparsely among high school rowers. Typically, our varsity eight would contain no more than two athletes who had rowed prior to college. This put us at an enormous disadvantage competitively. International recruiting had begun to blossom. We consistently faced elite international oarsmen who had come to the United States primarily to bolster a college team and secondly to get an education.

Nevertheless, there was something far more important that I gained on the Cornell rowing team. I learned what made rowing, and coxing, special. In college I fell in love with the sport and my position. I relished the opportunity to hop into a racing shell and get the most out of eight diverse individuals. The coxswain is a unique job in all of sport. It is somewhat comparable to a jockey or a quarterback, but there is nothing exactly like it. Coxing did not fulfill the physical needs I sought in sport, but the mental challenges far outweighed any negatives.

The coxswain's responsibilities to a crew are purely mental. The only physical requirement of the job is to maintain a low weight so oarsmen don't have to pull any unnecessary baggage. On the water, the cox is in charge of steering, strategy and motivation. The most important job of any cox is to allow his athletes to give their best possible performance. I believe that the necessary characteristics for a successful cox are focus, tenacity, leadership and calm under pressure.

We endured a variety of ups and downs during my four seasons at Cornell. We never managed to win the elusive national title, but we did restore a sense of respect and tradition to the program. In 1991 we finished fifth in the NCAA championships, and in 1992 we were fourth. I watched other crews win those races and wondered what separated us from them. I wondered what more I had to do to become a true champion. I always felt there was a winner inside ready to break out. I wanted to test my skills at a higher level. I wanted to try to be the best.

Three out of four summers during college I became involved with national rowing camps. After my freshman year, I spent six weeks in a development camp in Lake Placid, New York. The summer ended on a high note when our boat won a gold medal at the U.S. Olympic Festival in Oklahoma City, Oklahoma. I caught my first glimpse of elite national rowing and loved it. I was determined to press on.

My other two summer rowing experiences were far less enjoyable. In 1991 I was a late invite to the national team selection camp. This was my first trip to the big show. The top athletes would earn positions to represent the United States at the World Championships in Vienna, Austria. Our Cornell crew traveled to Henley, England that summer so I arrived late in Princeton. Tom Murray had convinced national team coach Kris Korzeniowski that I could compete with the other two coxswains, Tim Evans and Mike Moore. At Coach Korzeniowski's invitation, I flew back with to the United States to give it my best shot.

From the moment I stepped inside the Princeton boathouse, I never had a chance. Tim and Mike had proven themselves already, and I was an unknown element. There was a long-shot chance for another boat in the World Championships, a pair with coxswain including Rob Shepard, a world championships medallist. But through a bizarre set of circumstances, the other member of our potential crew backed out and left us high and dry. Rob Shepard went on to row in the U.S. eight in the Barcelona Olympics. I went back to my senior year of college.

I had another brief encounter with national team rowing after my senior year in 1992. Tom Murray had made the U.S. eight that raced in Vienna in 1991. He spent the following year training with Coach Korzeniowski for the Olympic team. After a variety of misfortunes, he had not made either of the camp's priority boats. There was one event left for selection, the pair with coxswain. Tom had formed a partnership with Jason Scott, and they were looking for a coxswain. They considered me as an option for one week. My hopes were high and I envisioned the thrill of Barcelona. But this, too, was not meant to be. I was the wrong guy at the wrong time. Sadly enough, Tom and Jason did not qualify for Barcelona either.

After leaving Cornell, I assumed that my coxing career was over. There was a bad taste in my mouth of unfulfilled potential, but I figured that fate had played itself out. I had been around the national team scene enough that if it were meant to be, I would have made it by now. I moved to Washington, D.C., took a job on Capitol Hill, and looked forward to building a "real life." It was a little over half a year before I was dragged back into the mix.

Chapter 1: 1993

I traveled to Philadelphia this past weekend to visit Tom Murray. Stayed at his apartment with Don Smith, a national team hopeful, and Ed Grose, a lightweight national team hopeful. To tell the truth their apartment is an absolute dump. Plywood and cardboard cover the front door, which only locks from the outside; the wall separating Tom and Ed's room is made entirely of cardboard; and some of the windows are boarded up to keep out the wintry cold air. They pay an astounding $50 per month! Actually they aren't paying anything this month because they are about to be evicted.

But, there was something much deeper than the house or the crap it was made of–the smell of dreams, of hope, of glory. These guys are putting their lives on hold in order to train for the chance to make the national team, and maybe one day the Olympic team. Here's the clincher–I was jealous of them.

I love my job here. I love my whole life here. Things could not be much better. I have a super job in the Senate. I live in a great apartment in my favorite city in the United States. Nearly every aspect of my life seems perfectly on track.

Then I look at Tom, Don, Ed, and the other rowers training up in Philly. I think, "Do those guys have guts or what?" They're willing to put it all on the line to see if they're good enough. I have never done that. I have never given up everything in order to see how good I really am.

What keeps me awake at night considering this insane idea is the fear of not knowing. I don't know how good I am. I don't know how good I could be. I don't know if I can make the national team. Hell, I don't know if I could ever make the weight–110 pounds for international coxswains. Granted I have played around with the idea and I have tried out before, but I have never sat on the line when the winner was crowned Champion of the World. I feel strongly that I do not have an answer to the ultimate question–am I good enough?

Something that also touches a raw nerve is the fact that two friends of mine, coxswains of the same age, Tim Evans and Mike Moore, put it all on the line. They went all the way to the Barcelona Olympics. They were willing to sacrifice their lives, drop out of school for a year and test themselves. They were rewarded for this sacrifice. They represented the United States in an Olympic Games.

Maybe I am way out of line here. Maybe Mike and Tim were leagues ahead of me. Maybe I have no business even putting myself anywhere near their level of coxing. After all, they had been on elite teams before (especially Juniors) when I had not. Maybe it is just a matter of destiny. They progressed through the system, and I was left in the dust. But at the same time fate has come back to me again now. It is a post-Olympic year and opportunity is knocking. Should I answer? I could say for the rest of my life that I coxed against Olympic coxes. Or I could take a greater risk and see what happens.

So what is the next step? Tom Murray called me tonight to tell me that he got a bunch of national team stuff in the mail today. Coxes need to send a resume to Indianapolis immediately for the eight camp. Otherwise it seems that all other boats will be selected by trials on June 4-6. Unfortunately that is not very far away. It is now March. The trials are in three months. If anyone is going to seriously train for the national team trials, they have to get going.

Maybe I am crazy to be thinking of all this nonsense, let alone writing about it. Honestly, this might be one huge waste of time. I have been on the periphery of the national team scene for a while now. Back in the summer of 1989, I lost a trial for the World University Games. In 1991, I went late to selection camp, got into a boat that had possibilities, but then fell apart.

In 1992, Tom tempted me with a tryout in a pair with for the Olympic Trials, but then they chose Jon Fish instead and still lost at the trials. I have been burned by this thing enough in the past. Why pull my sorry self out of the ruins for another chance to be crushed? Why do it now when I have so much going for me?

I'll tell you why.

Deep down I think I am a good cox. I think that I know how to motivate people, how to steer straight, and how to move a boat. I honestly think that I can compete with any cox in the country for any seat. If I don't believe that then it is not worth taking one more step. But I do believe it. I feel it. I, too, have dreams of glory and visions of victory. If I don't go all the way and sacrifice everything then I will never know if I could do it. I will never know if I had it in me.

I cannot help but think that these are the kinds of decisions that make great men. On the face of it, it probably seems like a totally crazy idea. In effect I would be giving up everything I have for the chance to have the opportunity to try out for the national team. Maybe I am stupid to consider this whole thing and maybe nothing will ever evolve anyway. Everything is one huge IF right now. But this situation could possibly be a defining moment in my life. This could be a life-determining decision.

For the next month and a half, Tom kept me apprised of developments with national team training. I always expressed an interest but never really thought about going through with any action. I simply did not think I could bring myself to give up all that I had worked for professionally to return to rowing. A late night phone call changed that.

The shrill ring of the telephone snapped the silence within my Arlington, Virginia apartment. After putting in too many twelve hour plus days at work, I was in search of a night of catch-up sleep that had been disturbed. Angrily I picked up the phone wondering who could be calling near midnight. "Hello," I mumbled.

"Yes. Steven Segaloff, please?" a British voice asked from the other end.

"Yeah. Can I help you?" I replied in a tone that let this mystery man know he had caught me asleep.

"Hi Steven. This is Mike Spracklen." He didn't need to say another word. The name said it all. One of the greatest rowing coaches in the world, arguably the greatest of all time. Mike had coached Olympic champions in each of the last three Olympiads (1984, 1988 and 1992). In fact, Spracky was the original coach of the most famous oarsmen in the world today, Steven Redgrave. Redgrave is currently tied for the record with consecutive Olympic gold medals in four Olympiads, and he is going for five in Sydney 2000. During the spring of 1993, Mike had been lured away from Canada to take charge of the American squad. Now he had called my house to ask me to cox.

I snapped to attention. In the next few moments, Mike told me about a lack of coxswains for the U.S. National Rowing Team. He asked if I was interested. There must have still been plenty of cobwebs in my head because my reply was no. There was too much going on at work. The timing wasn't right. I just could not do it.

The whole conversation lasted less than five minutes. By the time I returned the receiver to its cradle, I sat wide-awake in a state of total confusion. What had been a restful night of sleep ten minutes ago turned into hours of discomfort, indecision and frustration. I turned to my journal as a way to collect my thoughts.

Tuesday May 4, 1993   *Arlington, VA*

It's around midnight, and I'm tossing and turning so badly that I fear if I don't write, sleep is not going to come. I've been mulling over this rowing thing for over a week now and it is starting to wear me down. Tonight Spracklen called to invite me to the camp to choose the eight for Duisburg, Germany in a couple of weeks. I knew that this camp was happening, but had decided previously not to attend. Now that I've talked to Spracklen I feel like an idiot.

Soon after I hung up the phone and declined it occurred to me that I just passed up a chance for my best opportunity to get a foothold on the national team. I pretty much gave up a chance to go to Germany to race with the preliminary national team. What an idiot. Spracklen asked me if I could make the weeklong trip to Duisburg starting two weeks from yesterday. I explained to him that I was committed to my full-time job, but that I am interested in quitting in order to try out this summer. We briefly discussed the future camp situation and that was that. I feel like hell.

In closing, let me say that I need to figure this thing out one-way or the other because it is turning me into a wreck: at home, at work, anytime. Maybe I just need to make a decision and stick with it. I don't know where to go for answers.

After an evening of horrible sleep, I awoke the next morning, stumbled into the shower, and went through the motions of going into my office on Capitol Hill. Since graduating from Cornell University eight months earlier I had worked for Senator Joe Biden on the Senate Judiciary Committee. Minutes after sitting down and beginning a normal day of work, I realized the previous night's monumental mistake. When the Olympic coach calls and asks if you are interested it's not really a question. It is a summons. In less than five minutes, Spracklen had sunk the hook deep into my psyche. By now there was no chance of return.

Within an hour I approached my boss on the Committee, Chris Putala. Chris was one of Senator Biden's top aides in the Drug/Crime Unit, a position he attained as a perfectionist who demanded a similar commitment to the job from his disciples. This was the same committee that had fought many battles during my short stay there, including Anita Hill, Zoe Baird, and the Waco, Texas fiasco. During my brief tenure with the Committee it was not uncommon for me to work fourteen-hour days. In comparison, I did not think he would look too kindly on a request for leave of absence to sit in a boat. To my great surprise, everyone on the Committee was stunned by the opportunity. They all but packed my bags to wish me good luck. It took until lunch to make all the proper arrangements. I accepted a leave of absence to pursue my dream. I would try out for the national team after all.

Training camp did not actually start for nearly a week. Eight days after Spracklen's phone call I pulled my car into the Rutgers University boathouse in New Brunswick, New Jersey. Training camp had just begun the day before so I hadn't missed much. What I really missed was on-the-water experience since I hadn't been in a boat in over six months. "What the hell am I doing?" I asked myself for the umpteenth time that day. But another voice cautioned me to relax, step inside the boathouse, and see what fate had in store.

Many of America's boathouses are beautiful works of architecture that sit on picturesque lakes. Rutgers is an exception to that rule. The boathouse is a small, dingy building that abuts the polluted Raritan River. Amid this gloomy scene I entered my house of dreams. I could never have been ready for the events that followed.

Some of the faces inside were familiar, particularly that of my best friend Tom Murray. Tom was the driving force behind my return to the sport, so I instantly approached him to find out the latest scoop. Although Spracklen made the initial call, I had to thank Tom for suggesting my name. Tom was a year ahead of me at Cornell and always the stud of our team. He had rowed in the 1991 World Championships, but after a disappointing training year he had failed to make the 1992 Olympic team in Barcelona. Convinced that his potential had not been reached, Tom trained harder than ever in 1993 in the hopes of becoming a power for the 1996 Olympics.

Tom's words were brief, but positive. Camp had hardly begun and the other coxswain had not yet arrived. "Just relax and do your best. Don't worry about it." Easy for him to say since he had been training all year. My ass was on the line.

A few minutes later a small, older gentleman walked through the door. He looked quiet, unassuming, and maybe even frail. My first impression was that he was like Mr. Magoo from the cartoons. I would soon learn that this image was his first means of defense. Although he looked like a lamb, in reality he was a lion. He had as strong a desire to win as any person on earth. In the next few years, he would teach me as much as anyone ever had in life. His wisdom was profound, his commitment was limitless, and his desire was contagious. After we finished competing for Mike, no one would doubt that he contributed as much to our success as any one who sat in the boat.

We shuffled in our seats as Spracklen began his talk. Immediately my perception of a delicate, elderly gentleman vanished as his personality took over. He insisted on being called "Mike," rather than "Coach." He talked softly and would not hesitate through interruptions. His speech went along as planned and if you wanted to miss the message, it was your loss. Style was as important as substance in Mike's opening remarks. His point was simple but penetrating. He was here to lead the American men's eight to victory in Atlanta in 1996. If you were willing to follow him along that journey, the choice was yours.

I can't say what the others were thinking, but I was shocked to even hear mention of Atlanta. At that given moment, the 1996 Summer Olympics were the farthest thing from my mind. It was May 1993 in a small, crowded boathouse in New Jersey. I was simply hoping to make it through the afternoon. But already Mike had planted a seed in all of our heads: nothing in the next four years would matter more than that one race. Period. A few more words on the training program for the upcoming week, and we set out on the water.

Since it was my first time back in a coxswain's seat in months, I was scared stiff. This was not just any old practice. I was guiding the top rowers in the country through a practice with one of the world's greatest coaches. It was like playing pick-up with Jordan and Shaq while John Wooden ran the session.

I stepped into the boat and looked at the stroke man, Mike Porterfield. I didn't know Mike personally, but had seen his picture in plenty of magazines as a perennial top athlete. Mike was a three-time national team member from 1989 to 1991, including the Male Athlete of the Year in 1991 following his silver medal performance in the World Championships. Unfortunately, a back injury stopped him short of his dream of a berth on the Olympic team. Like Tom, he was another guy hungry to get back to the top. Sitting in front of me, Mike showed off a world championships uniform. It was a typical unisuit composed of blue shorts and a white shirt with two slim diagonal stripes of blue and red. Albeit simple, the significance was not lost on me in the moment.

Once I stopped gawking at Mike's uniform, I began to reacquaint myself with the coxswain's seat. I grabbed hold of the ropes around my waist that controlled the direction of the shell. Steering is an integral part of the coxswain's job, and at the national team level it was assumed to be done perfectly. Due to wind, tides, or other factors a boat does not simply go straight. Steering an eight requires the coxswain to make constant subtle changes, so as not to affect the delicate balance of the shell. As I took the ropes in my fingers, I prayed that it was like riding a bicycle.

I followed Spracklen's program and took the crew through their paces. Spracklen described the workout to me before we got on the water, which allowed him to watch instead of talk throughout practice. Communication was my responsibility and it would be the most important factor in my selection. We started off with a warm-up for about twenty minutes before getting into a few "pieces" of work. For the most part, I tried to use as few words as possible. "Stick to the point, communicate what needs to be done and then watch," I thought. Rather than acting as a know-it-all, I thought it best to ease my way into the situation.

A coxswain's respect in the boat is directly tied to what he says and how he says it. Had I waltzed right in and talked all day, guys would have sent me packing. Instead, I sat quietly while watching the athletes, listening to the coach, and trying to get a better understanding of everything around me. My first day of training with the crew would be best described as uneventful.

Early that evening my competition arrived: Jeff Gurrola, a coxswain from the Pennsylvania Athletic Club, Penn AC for short. For decades, Penn AC had produced some of our nation's best rowers. Philadelphia was a popular training spot, and Penn AC was driven by another of rowing's great characters, Ted Nash. Ted was an Olympic gold medallist in 1960 in Rome, who has since been involved, either competing or coaching, in every other summer Olympiad since. Ted's coaching style stems from his military background. Gruff like a drill sergeant, he inspires his charges through loud, staccato bursts. This is nearly the polar opposite of quiet, diplomatic Mike Spracklen. Jeff Gurrola had been coxing at Penn AC for nearly a year now and part of me was already convinced that his education under Ted Nash would send me back to D.C. before the people at work would miss me.

Spracklen asked Jeff to take the boat in the morning so that we could compare coxswains. Jeff had just returned from a competition in Italy with some of the Penn AC athletes, including a few who were in the eight he steered that morning. Over the hum of the motor, I could not hear a thing Jeff said to the crew, but I somehow convinced myself that he was taking me to school. The only thing I could notice was that he talked a lot, which must have meant he knew what he was doing. Jeff made the mistake of trying to take over a situation that was not his for the taking. By throwing out orders left and right, the guys started getting frustrated and not paying attention.

Meanwhile, Spracklen asked me to drive the coach's launch while he focused on the crew. My first time in this position, I got off to an auspicious beginning. The Raritan River is tidal, and practice took place while

the tide was going out. Spracklen was vaguely familiar with the shallow
spots along the waterway. Every now and then, he would caution me to
move more toward the center of the river. In one instance, while I was
probably planning my route back to Washington, Mike gave me a warning
I did not heed. Half a minute later I had driven the launch onto a sandbar
and thrown the engine in the air. "That's the last straw," I thought. "If I
wasn't cut before he'll do it now for sure."

But Spracklen's reaction remained totally placid. He must have
sensed the fear in my eyes. He calmly replaced the engine in the water
and guided me to deeper waters. After letting me know I had not paid
attention to his admonition, we were on our way again. That was that.

There was another practice that afternoon, in which I coxed the eight
again, another uneventful outing. Little did I know that I would soon
find out how quick and harsh selection could be. After the boat was
returned to its place in the boathouse Spracklen announced that we
would have "a gathering." Sounded innocent enough.

He told us that USRowing was under a deadline to put names of athletes on airline tickets for the next week's trip to Germany. Therefore we
would have to decide tonight on a few contested seats. The first order of
business was the coxswains. Mike asked, "Jeff and Steve, could you leave
the room so we could talk about you?"

"That was pretty straightforward," I thought as I walked into a
nearby room. "Just a few minutes of waiting in here and it will be all
over. Then I can go back to D.C., know that I gave it a shot, and get on
with a real life."

Jeff and I exchanged pleasantries for the few minutes we sat there
wondering what the future held. He talked about Italy for a while, and
his tone sounded as if this procedure was just a formality. At that point,
I started to re-think my own position. "Why be so passive?" my ego
roared. "Who is this guy to think I'm just some chump he can forget
about? I hope those guys pick me. I can do this. I know I can."

Shortly thereafter, Mike walked through the door. He asked me to leave so that he could speak with Jeff alone. "Why?" I thought to myself, stunned but still obeying. "Holy shit," I realized upon entering the main meeting room. "I pulled this off." Tom was right there with a high-five for support. I was on my way to Germany.

We still had five days to prepare in New Jersey. This was my first taste of life in the big leagues of rowing. I was ready for the sneaker contracts, the corporate sponsors and the cash incentives. But rowing's big leagues are not quite the equivalent of the lowest levels of America's most popular sports. While even the most minor leagues of professionals enjoy basic amenities like hotels or food, our existence was as Spartan as you could imagine. Forget the big money and endorsements. I joined my teammates at one of the nearby Rutgers oarsman's house. We slept on couches and dined on cereal, peanut butter, and macaroni and cheese. Through these types of hardships, we were more inclined to bond together and work for every inch of ground we could gain.

As the week progressed, I learned more about the other oarsmen in the crew. The squad for the 1993 Duisburg regatta included Jon Brown (JB), Fred Honebein, John Moore, Tom Murray, Mike Peterson, Will Porter, Mike Porterfield, and Don Smith. A few things were remarkable about this crew. First, the guys were huge. JB, John Moore, Will Porter and Don Smith are each at least 6'6", and the other four were taller than 6'2". All this height translated into boat speed because longer limbs necessarily mean more leverage with an oar against the water.

Apart from size, the character of the crew was hard-working, but fun-loving. Most of the guys had been on the outside looking in at previous national teams. This was a great opportunity to show America's new head coach that we could form the nucleus of the next Olympic crew. Surprisingly, four members of that initial Duisburg crew–JB,

Fred, Don and I—would remain together almost every step of the way through Atlanta.

Throughout our days of training, we fed off each other's intensity. Spracklen worked the squad hard, not just physically, but mentally. There is only so far you can take any team in one week, particularly in a sport highly dependent upon technique. But what you couldn't teach in terms of mechanics, you could certainly teach in terms of philosophy. Here was where Spracklen was unbeatable.

Looking ahead to Germany we were about to face the toughest crews in the world, most of them long on experience. Spracklen knew how tough the competition would be so he worked hard to instill a confident, positive attitude amongst the crew. Planting little seeds throughout the week, he allowed us to believe in our capabilities and ourselves. Realistically, we would have little chance facing recent Olympic medallists. But if we could achieve a level of confidence in each other, that was the kind of lasting quality that could carry a team through a season. As the week ended, we took great steps mentally and were ready to take on the world.

Sunday May 16, 1993　　　　　　　　　　*New Brunswick, NJ*

It's the eve of our flight to Germany and it has taken less than a week to get back to the same old routine. On the whole, I'm pretty excited about my situation. One week ago I was in my apartment realizing that my career was over, and tonight I've got a ticket to race at Duisburg for the U.S. against the best crews in the world. I'm not that nervous yet because I'm psyched to travel to Europe with this group of guys. We've been having fun together and the boat is going quite fast. We ended our workout today on a really good note and we're all happy with the boat speed. We have two more workouts tomorrow before we leave, and then it's onto Duisburg.

When we arrived in Duisburg, Germany I found myself sharing a small double room with one of the world's greatest rowing coaches. The guys each paired off with a friend from the crew, which left Spracklen and me as roommates. The idea of sharing a tiny, barren room in a far-away land with a rowing legend made me nervous as hell. Hardly two weeks out of my office, and now I was bedroom buddies with a man I hardly knew.

Spracklen must have sensed the nerves of the entire crew because that first night in Germany he took us out for a few beers. The theory was that a beer or two would help us fall asleep more easily. The reality was that lounging around a pub gave everyone the chance to relax and shake off the tension of our inaugural international competition. By the second round of drinks, we had all loosened up. After a few crude jokes and some otherwise typical locker room banter we had forgotten the pressures of racing. For the time being, we were just an obnoxious group of loud Americans causing a ruckus at a European bar.

While walking back to the hotel I noticed that although Spracklen was a hell of a coach, he was no drinker. Two beers had given him a pretty good buzz and within moments of opening our door, he fell asleep on his bed fully dressed. It was then that I learned that his ability to fall asleep quickly was matched by an ability to snore loudly. While I brushed my teeth before bed, I took another look at the crazy scene around me. This can't possibly be real, I mused. I threw the pillow over my head to drown out the noise coming from my roommate. This was life on the road with a legend.

Duisburg was the season's first international world cup race, a series of which would lead up to the World Championships. Essentially this was the first important international race since the 1992 Summer Olympics in Barcelona, Spain. Duisburg was the first step of the new quadrennial, which would end in Atlanta in 1996.

At the Barcelona Olympics, Canada won the men's eight led by none other than our current coach. Romania finished second in Barcelona by one-quarter of a second. Huge, burly men, they came back with a vengeance in 1993. As athletes, they lived better lives than average Romanian citizens. It behooved them to continue to compete as long as possible. They returned to Duisburg to begin their journey to the top. Such a narrow loss motivated their oarsmen to keep going.

In Barcelona, the Canadians had scored a major upset by winning the gold medal. Prior to their victory, the German eight had created a dynasty in the event. They captured the gold medal in the 1988 Olympics in Seoul and proceeded to win world championships in 1989, 1990, and 1991. To falter in Barcelona was not just an upset, it was a blow to German domination. Spracklen often said that Canada's win was a once in a lifetime opportunity. "If they had rowed that race six times Germany most likely would have won five of them." When 1993 came around, the German rowing federation sought to recapture their status as kings of the world. They lured most oarsmen back with promises of significant salaries, heretofore unheard of in the sport. What better place to re-ignite the German tradition of winning the men's eight than the heart of the Rhineland, Duisburg.

Duisburg is a small, industrial city within an hour of Frankfurt. As we began our first international trip, I was excited to visit a new country and maybe check out a few of the sights. I had never visited Germany and thought this might be a good chance to take in a few tourist spots. Immediately, I learned how these rowing trips would work. You see a lot of the water, the hotel and the commute back and forth, but that's about it. For the next few years, we would journey to many exciting places–St. Petersburg, Russia; Prague, The Czech Republic; Buenos Aires, Argentina; London, England; and so on. My friends would marvel at how frequently I used my passport and got to see the world. Little did they know that most of these trips provided virtually no sightseeing. If we were lucky, we would have one free afternoon per trip to quickly sprint through a local museum or tourist spot.

Most of my first trip with the U.S. team was spent getting to know the guys. I came from nowhere to become a member of the crew, and my job in the boat demanded a cohesive relationship with the athletes. Many of the important qualities of a good coxswain require a close relationship with the crew members. The most important task for the coxswain is to get the best out of each oarsman. You constantly try to pull eight men together towards a common goal. When race day comes, you scream your guts out at these guys to pull until their hands bleed. Before asking for such intensely personal requests, it helps to establish a rapport built upon trust and respect. I certainly could not expect to build a lifetime's relationship in one week, but you had to start somewhere.

Friday May 21, 1993   *Duisburg, Germany*

Tomorrow is it–race day. We've prepared ourselves as best as possible and we're all pretty excited about tomorrow. Having Coach Spracklen certainly helps. His positive, winning attitude gives us great hope that we can truly compete.

I'm very excited for tomorrow, and surprisingly not that nervous. I only just started to get nervous when I sat down to write this entry. We've got a solid race plan and I feel ready to execute it properly. That's the best I can do. If we race to our full potential, we have the ability to show the rowing world that the U.S. is a power to be feared.

Tomorrow morning there are two heats of four, each with three to qualify for the afternoon final. Sunday there will be another set of heats and finals. What's fun is that we really don't know how fast we are. We've done a few timed pieces, and Mike says we're producing some very fast times. But what do we know? All we can do is get off strong and try to kick it down the course as fast as we can.

So that's the plan. Now it's time to show everyone what we've got. The next two days of racing are very important because we'll set the precedent for U.S. men's sweep rowing in the Spracklen era. Everything doesn't hinge on tomorrow, but it would be great to get off on the right foot.

When race day came around our confidence abounded. We had a boat full of big, strong guys; we knew how to row; we had the best coach in the world; and after all, we were Americans. We could win. Spracklen padded our confidence, but was also cautious that we would become too proud too quickly. The night before the regatta he told me he would be "shocked" if we won.

Saturday May 22, 1993   *Duisburg, Germany*

My first high-caliber international race is under my belt, and I think it went quite well. In a race of four, with three to qualify, we finished second. The Dutch beat us by three-quarters of a length, and we killed Russia and Poland. In the other final, Germany won quite easily, Romania second and Britain third. So the final will be: Germany, Romania, Britain, Dutch, U.S. and Russia. The toughest crews look like Germany and the Dutch; Romania could also be solid. I don't expect too much of a challenge from Britain or Russia.

It's amazing to think that we're right in the thick of it all. Two weeks ago, Germany beat the Dutch by a deck so they seem to have comparable speed. We all feel like we can tag the Dutch, so why not Germany also? Hell, we could win this thing! Mike is not that impressed. He said he would be "amazed" if we win.

I thought I did an okay job. I wasn't spectacular, but there was no need to be. We got the job done. Still, I need to have a better race if we're to win this afternoon. I need to get it revving in the third 500 and call a good sprint. It's very important to keep cool the whole time. Let's get 'em.

[Post-final.] Things didn't work out as we expected. Nevertheless, it was a rather successful race. Germany won by two seconds over Romania, who was six-tenths of a second ahead of the Dutch. We were about 1.5 seconds behind the Dutch in fourth place. Britain was more than two seconds behind us, and Russia was about five seconds behind them. Before the race Spracklen said he would be excited if we were overlapping the Germans. We all thought we were capable of that and more. Unfortunately, we fell short of that goal because we were a bit of open water behind the Germans. Part of that had to do with the fact that we had hoped to win and we were pissed about that in the second half of the race.

We were all a bit frustrated because we had hoped to do so well, but Mike read us like a book. In our meeting this evening he stressed the fact that it's great to have high expectations, but we can't expect to whip the Germans—a boat full of World Champions and Olympic bronze medallists.

Now we have the opportunity to do it again tomorrow. It's going to be tough, but it will give us the immediate opportunity to take revenge on the Dutch. We can beat these guys and it would be fantastic to do it. That's where we've got to focus our attention.

Sunday May 23, 1993   *Duisburg, Germany*

This morning we raced in a heat to qualify for the most important final of the weekend. We faced Germany, Czechoslovakia and Poland with two to qualify. The Czechs and the Poles were never a factor, so we could have qualified easily, but we wanted to push our luck against Germany. From the start it was clear that the guys wanted to go after Germany and push them as hard as possible. In short, we had something to prove after yesterday.

It wasn't a great race, but we certainly held our own. The Germans had a half-length by the 500m, but we kept pressing. We would move a few seats and they would push back out. They did just enough to maintain a comfortable distance. A few times I caught them looking at us with an expression that said, "Will you cut it out? We're both going to qualify!" At the finish, they crossed the line 1.2 seconds ahead of us, a margin we were very happy about. We didn't have any delusions of grandeur about the final. We just wanted to put out a top performance. It looked to be a very fast final, and we were prepared to show our stuff. Lane 1 USA, 2 Poland, 3 Netherlands, 4 Germany, 5 Romania, 6 Denmark.

[Sunday's Final.] We got off the line quite well, the best so far of the regatta. Our first 500m was strong and we were right in the hunt. The results show us only three-quarters of a second behind the leader, Romania. Before the race, we decided to race the Dutch. We saw them as a beatable crew, and a win against them would make us all happy. We kept thumping on the second 500m and a great race was shaping up. We were trading back and forth with the Dutch: one seat up, one seat down, one seat up, and so on. Our previous third 500s had been a bit wishy-washy, so we really wanted to go after it. As we crossed the half-way mark, I took a look around, and lo and behold, the Germans were right there. I was just a seat or two off the German stroke. Romania was up a bit on them, and we felt good. The third 500m went pretty well, and we cranked into the sprint still in a position to win. Germany began their massive sprint, so they started to pull away. Still, we were neck and neck with the Dutch. It was getting very loud as we approached the grandstand, and we kept firing it up. Our finishing stroke rates were the highest we had gone yet—beyond 40, 41, 42, up to 42 ½ strokes per minute, but we just couldn't move our bow out far enough. We lifted for twenty strokes, then for fifteen, and we were still even, maybe even a bit up on the Dutch. We kicked it up for the last twenty (up for ten, then ten again). Despite our rise in rate, the Dutch somehow found another gear. They moved out to a 1.4 second lead over us. They even came close to nipping Romania.

We were a bit upset that we couldn't overcome the Dutch, and we still missed the dreaded overlap on the Germans because they had us by four seconds. But I was very proud of our performance. More importantly, the guys were pleased and that let me feel as though I did a good job.

It's now after 12:30am on Monday morning before our departure and I should be getting some rest. Yet I have to end with what looks to be a final decision. This evening we had a blow-out meeting to discuss the next two weeks, most importantly the upcoming national team trials. There is a four with coxswain being formed that looks to be quite strong: Mike Peterson, Will Porter, Tom Murray and John Brown. Based on my performance here, I have been asked to join the crew. It appears that there will be very little competition, maybe a Penn AC four. Even if this four doesn't pan out for whatever reason, I am confident that I would at least get invited to the eight selection camp. Better yet, after speaking with Spracklen I am comfortable (maybe I shouldn't be) that I can reach the show this year. If I do this, I am about 90% sure that I will make the jump to San Diego next fall for full-time training.

We headed back to the United States in positive spirits. Everything had not gone perfectly, but we felt as though we had tons of room to grow. We had mixed it up with the best in the world and held our own. There was plenty of hope for the season ahead.

The first round of trials for the 1993 U.S. National Team were held in Mercer County, New Jersey a few weeks after Duisburg. Our four had spent the interim training in Philadelphia, and we were excited about the opportunity to be named to the national team. For many sports, you would expect a crowd of thousands or at least hundreds to come watch the nation's best attempt to represent their country at a World Championships. In our case, we were lucky if all of our own parents showed up. Attendance at these events was miserable.

To say the regatta was low-key would be a tremendous understatement. Excluding competitors, coaches and officials it would be realistic to say there were thirty people watching. Yet these races were the first round of trials that would create the 1993 U.S. National Rowing Team at the upcoming World Championships. Rowing careers were on the line.

The trials exemplified the beauty of the sport of rowing. It would be great to race in front of thousands of adoring fans, but that was not what rowing is about in our country. In our event, the four with coxswain, two boats sat on the starting line. At one end of the lake ten young men (two four man boats and two coxswains) sat awaiting their destiny. Each had trained hard and prepared for the moment. We sat quietly for the few minutes before the start and waited patiently for the fury ahead. In minutes, we would learn our fate. It did not matter that America was not watching to see who would go to the World Rowing Championships. The men and women on the starting line had enough hope and desire in their hearts to account for thousands of fans.

Because it was the year after an Olympics, even the competition was sparse. The eight from Duisburg had broken down into three separate boats, a four with coxswain, a pair with coxswain and a pair without coxswain. Spracklen would choose the national team eight later in the summer from a large pool of athletes, including college all-stars. This round of trials was to recognize the smaller boats.

The trials themselves turned out to be largely anticlimactic. The regatta format was best of three racing where the winners also had to satisfy a time standard in order to prove their worth as international competitors. All three crews from the Duisburg eight won their opening races and qualified under the time standard.

We would still have to race the next morning to make it official, but that was pretty much a formality. For all intents and purposes, we had earned spots on the U.S. National Rowing Team. In my boat, a coxed four including Jon Brown, Tom Murray, Mike Peterson, and Will Porter, emotions were very high. Tom had been on the squad in 1991, and JB and Will were on the Pan Am Team the same year. But now we were the first ones in the door in 1993 and nothing could stop us en route to Atlanta in 1996.

Friday June 4, 1993   **Princeton, NJ**

This afternoon I attained a goal I have held in incredibly high regard for many years. After nearly ten years of coxing, today I brought myself within one very small step of earning a spot on the U.S. National Team to represent our country in the World Championships in Racice, the Czech Republic in late August.

On the ride home from the course with Tom, I actually felt like crying. I can't explain the emotions that ran through my body. After trying and failing so many times, who would have thought it would actually happen? This afternoon that dream is very close to reality. In order to ensure our positions, all we have to do is beat the Penn AC crew. Since we beat them by eighteen seconds today, I would say that's not a big hurdle.

After rowing, we all planned to have dinner together at the Olive Garden to celebrate. Our whole boat was going with Don Smith and Fred Honebein, who had just qualified in the pair. We all had a ball at dinner and enjoyed thinking about the fun summer ahead.

Spracklen joined us at the restaurant for a relaxing dinner. Since returning from Duisburg, we had spent the previous few weeks worrying about how things would work out for the remainder of the summer. After the afternoon's racing, all our questions were answered. As the coxed four and the pair we would train together throughout the summer, and maybe even go back to Europe for more racing experience. By the first week in September we would end up at the World Championships in the Czech Republic. We were set.

As we asked our waitress for the bill Spracklen changed the conversation. He began talking about the priority boats of the U.S. squad. The coxed four and the pair were good boats, but not premier boats. In fact, the coxed four was no longer an Olympic event. The eight was the key. After a brief speech, it was clear where Mike was headed. He asked the seven of us to decline our seats and try out for the eight next month. My jaw dropped to the ground.

We were floored. At that moment we had each achieved a life-long goal. By earning a seat on the national team, we had climbed to the top of a mountain. Now Spracklen wanted us to walk right back down only to have to climb up a steeper peak? You must be kidding me. He asked us to give up our seats in exchange for a chance at the eight. "You all should make it," he said, "but I can't guarantee it."

We sat around the dinner table for over an hour debating Mike's request. Undoubtedly we all wanted to be in the eight, but would it be worth sacrificing the guaranteed seats we currently held? The argument went back and forth for a while and we decided to sleep on it and resolve the issue in the morning. Besides, we still had to win another race before any decision could be made.

Saturday June 5, 1993   *Princeton, NJ*

As expected, we beat the other boat and officially qualified as the coxed four for the 1993 U.S. National Team. Surprisingly though, as we paddled back to the dock and returned to accept warm congratulations from family, friends and so on, we felt a little somber. We knew that we had a monumental decision in front of us. Everything was quite hectic for the first few hours on land. We had to take drug tests, fill out forms, etc. Then we gathered to decide our fate.

The five of us went to a corner with Coach Spracklen. We discussed, at length, the many issues involved in this decision. His point of view was that he wanted us in his eight and would like us to decline the four. He sympathized with the fact that we were giving up a guarantee, but considering that the eight is THE boat, he thought we would accept his offer. There were no absolutes about us being in the eight, but he did guarantee us that we would at least be in the top camp coxed four if any of us had to return for re-trials one month later.

We hemmed and hawed over this for several hours, but in the end we simply could not turn down the offer. We all felt that such a bold decision would show our commitment to the team, and furthermore a signal of our strength of trust in Coach Spracklen. I have no regrets about what we did. It sucks to think that I gave up a guarantee, but to be in the eight would be simply awesome. I must have faith that Spracklen wouldn't lead us down that road if he didn't really believe in our ability. Don and Fred won the straight pair trial, and they, too, declined the selection in order to try out for the eight.

The seven of us had sealed our fates. In hindsight, our decision was really a no-brainer. After a little over a month with this charismatic coach, we had resolved to hitch our hopes to his wagon. We would follow him anywhere. A few days later, we were off to Indianapolis for a two week training camp prior to the U.S. National Championship Regatta.

The two weeks we spent in Indianapolis training and racing for the 1993 U.S. National Championships are still among my fondest memories of my four-year experience. We had recently returned from Duisburg, and as a result of our modest success in Europe, our heads had quickly grown quite large. Most of the elite American rowing community descended upon the Midwestern town and we never missed an opportunity to tell people who we were and what we intended to do. We were Spracky's core group. He was a great coach, therefore we must be a great crew.

Wednesday June 16, 1993   **Indianapolis, IN**

We arrived in Indy last evening for the start of training camp. As for my situation, and that of the decliners, it still looks pretty good. Spracklen is not at all anxious to integrate us with the Pre-Elite rowers, who are mostly college all-stars. It seems like he's trying to insulate us from the group for now. It will be interesting to see how the week progresses for all of us. Because Spracklen is a new coach, everybody is a bit unsure about his plans for selection. On a personal note, I can't help but feel confident. It is this confidence that allows me to compete every day. There are four or five other coxes here, including Mikey Moore, the coxswain of the 1992 U.S. Olympic eight. I have no clue as to how Spracklen views the coxing situation or what he plans to do. I keep thinking in the back of my mind what he said at Mercer County, "I would love to have you cox the eight this summer."

On a different note, I have an important discovery to discuss related to my coxing technique. In fact, it's so important, so fundamental that I think (and hope) that it will positively affect my ability forever.

As with most important and significant ideas, this one is also very simple. It all started with a conversation I had with Tom Murray on our ride from Princeton to New York City. Last week, he was giving me some advice about coxing and he suggested that I be a little more "sympathetic" in the boat. As he put it, I should try to be a little more helpful, as opposed to being dictatorial.

I went for a long jog and started to think about what Tom had said. What I tried to do at first was put myself in the shoes of an elite oarsmen, someone who would be at selection camp trying out for the men's eight. It occurred to me that these guys would have little interest in a bossy cox who tried to control the crew every moment. I don't have to emphasize motivation much either because these guys will already be highly motivated on their own. A key tenet to this line of thought is that there is a huge change that must occur between college and elite level rowing—a change that could be fundamental to my success as a cox in the future.

It basically comes down to the needs of a crew. A college crew needs the discipline of a forceful cox who will take control all the time and really whip the crew through practice and into racing. An elite crew, on the other hand, is well-versed in the ideas of mental and physical preparation both on and off the water. The elite crew needs a cox who will most effectively carry out the coach's ideas, primarily technique. In my case, Spracklen certainly has a very particular philosophy about rowing and philosophy about technical rowing. My job is to mold the crew into one similar pattern of thought, not through loud yelling, but more through pure execution. I must add that another key to this new technique is a close watch of my tone of voice. Since this "epiphany" I have tried to be very helpful in the boat, as if I wanted to do my best to allow these guys to reach maximum performance.

Again, this is a simple idea. Help the oarsmen do their best, give them the best chance to make the team.

At this point, I began to deal with a demon that would haunt me throughout my involvement in international rowing–weight loss. The rules of international rowing required a minimum of 110 pounds (50kg) in the coxswain's seat. A minimum is established so that each crew will race with at least that much weight. If you want to have more weight than that, you are welcome to do so. However carrying any extra weight is only going to slow a crew down. The weight rule is the reason that coxswains are small. It was my task to come as close to 110 pounds as possible.

I had some experience with weight loss as a wrestler in high school, but this was far more dramatic. While working in Washington, D.C., I tipped the scales at 125 pounds. I could not drop 15 pounds, 12% of my body weight, overnight. I worked hard each day to lower my weight consistently and effectively. Little did I know how big this problem would become. For weeks already, my daily consumption had been drastically reduced. I had fought to weigh about 115, but struggled to maintain the necessary energy to last all day. It was hard to endure the

summer's heat while eating one pancake, a Power Bar and some fruit for
a whole day.

Wednesday June 23, 1993   **Indianapolis, IN**

*Suffice it to say that the eight we've formed for the national championships
is easily the fastest damned boat I've ever coxed in my life. We made two
changes by dropping Mike Porterfield and John Moore and inserting Willie
Castle and John Riley. When I sit in the stern and call for full pressure pieces
I feel like I'm driving a Ferrari. The boat is moving so quickly that I'm almost
afraid to touch the steering like the brakes of a race car. Duisburg was certainly a very fast boat, but there seems to be a new element here. Perhaps it
has to do with the environment of the National Championships.*

*Not only is it very fast, though, the boat is a lot of fun. I have a great
time with the guys, and we're all enjoying the hell out of going so fast. As
we were pulling out of the parking lot this morning in a car with the four
from trials, the radio blasted gangster-rap music, while people stared at
our egotistical behavior. Murray put his hands up, shrugged, and said,
"What can I say? We're fast." That seems to be the general sentiment.*

Thursday June 24, 1993   **Indianapolis, IN**

*The racing officially began today at the U.S. National Rowing
Championships. Although we didn't have a race, I spent a good part of the
day at the course. The highlight was the short time I spent talking with Terry
Paul, last summer's Olympic gold medal coxswain for Canada under Coach
Spracklen. Spracklen introduced me, and we had a good conversation.*

*We spent a few minutes talking about coxing under Spracklen, and I
found that part of the conversation to be revealing. Terry certainly didn't tell
me anything magical. There are no secrets that are the key to coxing for*

Spracklen. Instead, he reiterated the same ideas that I have heard over the past two months. The real key is to earn the trust and respect of the oarsmen.

What I found to be inspirational was when Terry told me how Spracklen would most likely want to cultivate a relationship with one coxswain and continue it through the Olympics. He figured that I had enough skill to get my foot in the door, and if I worked hard to continue our relationship in a positive way, the sky was the limit. He strongly encouraged me to stay by Spracklen's side and to learn as much as possible.

Terry also warned me that Spracklen would certainly test my own toughness. He told me about Mike putting intense pressure on the cox at times to elicit a firm method of decision-making and leadership. For example, Mike would drive the launch and camp out on the blades to ensure a dead straight course. Terry also told me of times that he felt like quitting when it got tough. But in the end, he found Spracklen to be the ultimate teacher, someone who led him to the Olympic gold medal.

At times in the course of our conversation, I found myself getting worried that I might not stand up to Spracklen's test. But then I realized that these were natural fears, the same ones Terry experienced, or any cox for that matter. Coxing for Spracklen is merely a continuation of a test of my own mental abilities. I've given plenty of thought to the rigors of coxing, and I'm certainly willing to go for it right now. There are many tremendous opportunities in the future of American rowing–World Championships, Goodwill Games, Henley Royal Regatta, and possibly the absolute ultimate, the Olympic Games. I feel that Spracklen will always give me a fair shake, and I hope that through diligence and perseverance I can reach the same pinnacle as Terry Paul after the summer of 1996.

Saturday June 26, 1993   ndianapolis, IN

Today was a big step in the right direction. Also a day to enjoy the fruits of our labor. This morning we won the U.S. National Championships in

*the elite men's coxed four. The other four had a strong line-up, including 1996 Olympians Scott Munn and coxswain Mikey Moore and national team hopefuls Jason Scott, Ted Murphy and Duncan Kennedy. The other boat was fired up to beat us and show that Spracky's group didn't deserve separate treatment. If we had faltered, it would have been bad news. This was their **only** race of the weekend, so it was certainly their sole focus. They felt as though they had plenty to prove to beat "the chosen ones." We were quite pumped up ourselves and we came through.*

We had a very good start and were immediately out to a three to four seat lead. At the 500m mark, we led by three seconds, and we extended our lead to four seconds by 1000m. Incidentally, what also made the win meaningful was the fact that the other boat knew our race plan. When we learned this before the race, it didn't even matter. We figured that we would simply go at them with our game plan and attack all the way. There was no reason to change our plans—we were the ones to fear. We kept the four to five second lead through the 1500m and held a bit of open water through the finish.

I was very proud of the guys because they really gave it their all. After the race Peterson and Murray could barely stand up. Meanwhile, Will and JB carried the boat into the rack alone. Afterward, it took Tom and Mike over half an hour to get to the drug testing station. It was very apparent that they gave this race every drop they had. It was a full pull.

I feel a big weight lifted off my shoulders now, and I'll be even more psyched if things work out tomorrow in the eight race. In order to keep succeeding I need to take things one day at a time. There's a huge future ahead for the United States men's sweep team, and right now I'm at the crest of that wave. Through careful attention to detail and a continued positive attitude, I'm confident that I can stay there.

As race week continued, though, a serious issue first raised its ugly head, sponsorship. In high-profile sports, such as basketball, baseball, football, and hockey, money is constantly at the center of attention.

One need only look at the frequency of labor disputes and lock-outs to see how important athlete compensation has become in the world of professional sports. Rowing is clearly not among these elite few, and as a result the sport struggles to find a balance. Athletes are expected to train full-time in order to develop their skills, but our governing body provides very little financial assistance. The traditional school of thought would be that we can't pay people to train because that would devalue the sport. Meanwhile, athletes have given up lucrative jobs after graduating from top universities, only to live at the poverty line. Since our crew in Indy was not the type to go quietly, a confrontation emerged.

In rowing, as with any other sport, people typically want to see the biggest, fastest events. Those same boats tend to receive the most publicity. Thus, as the men's heavyweight eight, we were likely to be covered more than anyone else by the media. While we prepared for the National Championships we realized early in race week that we had no team uniform. We knew that Champion International was the official sponsor of the National Team, so we asked USRowing if they could provide us with something to wear on race day. Their response was that we were not yet officially the national team, so they could not help us out.

When we raced at Duisburg our uniforms were bought at Kmart. We wore solid white T-shirts with American flag patches sewn on the chest. In my four years on the national team I received hundreds of pieces of gear. Above all else, I still cherish that simple T-shirt as my finest bit of clothing.

It bears pointing out that this initial action goes a long way towards the unprofessional state of the sport of rowing. We weren't asking for a million dollar signing bonus. We weren't asking for first class airplane tickets. We weren't even asking for money to put food on the table. All we asked for were some stupid T-shirts. Not only was this request incredibly small, it was in their best interest for the publicity of the sponsor. But in their infinite wisdom, USRowing denied our request.

"Okay," we responded. "But just so you know we're now going to look to a local establishment for support."

"Fine." was US Rowing's response, "Do whatever you like."

Throughout the week we had been eating at Puccini's Pizza, a restaurant we chose because it was five minutes from our accommodations. A few days before the eights race, we approached the manager and asked if they would cut us a break on the pizza and supply us with T-shirts to wear during the race. We were favored to win and also figured that the victory would more or less ensure our picture on the front of the Indianapolis newspaper. The manager took five seconds before agreeing and went to the storeroom for the shirts. We informed USRowing of our deal and again they seemed not to care. When race day finally came, it was quite a different story.

Our competition in the final was modest indeed. We faced two college all-star crews, a weak Canadian boat, and two throw-together boats. Based on our past performance in Europe, we were favored to win by at least a length of open water. As the race progressed, we got our first lesson in over-confidence. We blasted out to a one length lead in the first minute and never moved again. The top college all-star crew was thrilled to still have contact and we just sat there waiting for them to die. It never happened. We won by three seconds or so, but the victory was hollow to say the least. As the guys collapsed over their oars, they immediately knew we were in for trouble in the weeks to come. The mood was tense enough before the referee's launch zoomed over to our shell.

The race was not over for more than two minutes before a motor boat pulled alongside our crew. An official looking gentleman stood up and began speaking. "Congratulations on your win," he said quickly, and then moved onto his main point. "Fellas, I've got some shirts here I'd like you to wear onto the awards dock." He held up a "USA Rowing" shirt. "We've got a million-dollar sponsor on the shore. It just wouldn't be right if you boys arrived with those pizza shirts on." He started to hand me the shirts assuming that it would be as easy as that to make his case.

Suddenly from all over the boat there arose a chorus of disagreement. The oarsmen were pissed off at this guy, USRowing, or anyone else bothering us at the time. The responses were loud and plentiful, "Fuck you, asshole!…We're not wearing shit!…You had your chance!…Get the hell out of here!"

The official, who turned out to be the Treasurer of USRowing, was taken aback to say the least. Little did he know that nobody in our crew was going to kowtow to any guy in a blazer who said that we had to do something. In our minds, we had given USRowing the opportunity from the start but they didn't want to help. We made a commitment to Puccini's to support their restaurant.

The official, however, was not prepared to take no for an answer. After ten minutes more of arguing, he left the shirts with me in the stern of the boat. I passed them back to the guys, but most of the shirts were left in the bottom of the shell. We rowed towards the medal dock where a loud, clear voice called out from the official's finish tower, "You men are a disgrace to your sport." To this day, none of us have forgotten or forgave this incredibly uninformed remark.

As we climbed out of the boat to accept our national championship medals most of us made sure to mug for the camera. We proudly displayed the Puccini's shirts. To appease USRowing we briefly posed for one quick set of photographs with the USA shirts. However, we were all thrilled to see that the picture that appeared in the next day's *Indianapolis Star* showed off the Puccini's emblem.

Far more important than the T-shirt scandal was our failure to race to potential. Moments before our final in Duisburg Mike had ended our boat meeting by telling us the golden rule of racing, "Don't stick." His theory was that when crews are racing there should always be some movement, either backwards or forwards. If two boats were going along neck and neck for an extended period of time that proved that both crews were comfortable in their current position. In Indianapolis, we had "stuck" with a far less talented college all-star crew. Leading by one length, we sat there and waited for them to break. Instead of responding with an attacking rhythm, we were too content with that margin of victory.

After two racing experiences, our profile emerged. Racing at Duisburg with a nothing to prove mentality, we performed adequately and developed an ego. Racing at Indianapolis with a bloated ego, our performance suffered. The way to diminish the ego problem was quickly solved in Princeton. Mike threw everyone back in a selection pool. We would each have to prove ourselves anew.

Upon arriving in Princeton, it became clear that the honeymoon was over. Gone were the days of guys hanging out with Spracky in a laid back atmosphere. Princeton developed into a grueling six-week camp designed to teach everyone new limits in an old sport. Up to this point, Mike had needed to inspire confidence in a group of unknowns. He had needed to build us up in order to face the long odds in Germany. In Princeton, the dynamic was quite different. Now his task was to select the top eight out of twenty or so hopefuls. He had to assert his authority into building his first American eight.

The athlete pool at the 1993 Princeton camp was a mixture of talent that was diverse in every way: age, experience, background, and so on. There were athletes from every stage of their career—guys who were on their last legs compared to kids still competing in college who had never rowed internationally.

At one end of the spectrum there were a number of proven athletes, most of them Olympians, who represented the leftovers from the past quadrennial. All had competed successfully in previous years, but they now carried with them the burden of re-proving their abilities to a new coach. This group included Mike Teti, America's reigning rowing legend, three-time Olympian and 1987 world champion; John Parker, stroke of the American eight in Barcelona; and, John Riley, a two-time Olympian with one of rowing's brashest personalities.

On the other hand there were a number of younger, more naive, and hungry guys. They didn't know how good they could be, but they were ready to give up everything trying to find out. These were the all-stars of their respective college programs, who hoped to gain a foothold in Spracky's new stable of horses: Jon Brown from Boston University; Fred Honebein from Cal-Berkeley; Tom Murray from Cornell; and, Don Smith from Syracuse. Younger still were a few current college stars who were good enough to compete internationally, notably, Willie Castle from Penn, Jamie Koven from Brown, and Ted Murphy from Dartmouth. These guys had already won so much in their collegiate careers that they hardly knew what losing was like. Ironically, as the camp progressed, the older, seasoned athletes moved toward the bottom of the ladder, overtaken by a youthful spirit that would form the core of the 1993 eight, and in turn the 1996 Olympic eight.

There were three coxswains at the 1993 selection camp: Mikey Moore, Walt Mullen, and myself. Walt had already been chosen as the cox of the pair with crew, so the seat in the eight was between Mikey and me. In terms of experience, I was the hands down loser. Mikey coxed the U.S. four with in 1991 and the eight at the Olympics in Barcelona. He had been on the line in some of the world's most important races and that record alone gave him a sizable advantage. Additionally, Mikey's personality made him an even more formidable opponent. He grew up on the legendary Schuylkill River in Philadelphia, a factory for national team coxswains. There are so many crews competing for space on the small river that anyone who battles up and down its shores for a few seasons gains immeasurable experience in becoming some kind of tough guy. As a result you will find that most coxswains who come out of Philly already think they're better than anyone else.

Mikey was a proven leader on the water, and he knew the ins and outs of earning a seat as well as anybody. At the elite level, less separates one coxswain from another, so politics can become a major issue. Wasting no time, Mikey went right to work on the top guys to gain their trust and develop a relationship in order to assert himself as a member of the eventual eight. In my favor, though, Mikey had made a mistake back in May by choosing to finish the season at Temple University instead of attending the Duisburg camp in Rutgers.

By electing to stay in school, Mikey sent Spracklen a signal that he was not willing to make the extra sacrifice to try out for the national team just yet. His decision gave me enough of an opening to establish myself as the coxswain of a new group of oarsmen. What Mikey had in career experience I matched in interpersonal relations with this new crop of athletes. Mikey may have been the man for Barcelona, but by Princeton I had put in nearly two months with the top athletes, and more importantly, the coach. From the beginning Spracklen told me I had "a lot to learn." But as far as I was concerned that gap was narrowing by the day.

Whether you had been on ten national teams or none, every oarsmen who climbed the ladder of success at any level arrived in Princeton expecting to go through a typically American selection camp. Selection is the nasty business of deciding the members of the top boat. Each coach has his own specific methods, but in the United States at all levels, the dominant method is *seat racing*.

Seat racing is the unique rowing experiment that most programs use to choose their top oarsmen. Two crews are sent on the water in a specific line-up to race for a pre-determined amount of time for an indefinite number of pieces of work, usually just called "pieces." The boats race and the results are noted. After the first piece, the coach announces a man for man change amongst the crews, for example, Bob switches with Frank. The crews re-race for the same amount of time, and the results are compared. By analyzing the margins of victory between the switches, coaches determine which oarsman won his seat race.

Even a cursory analysis of this process will show you that it is fraught with inconsistencies. Seat racing has far too many variables involved to produce definite results. Changes in wind direction, water conditions and athlete psychology play too big a role to make seat racing a fair process. During a seat racing session, some athletes spend more time trying to second guess what the coach is thinking rather than concentrating on their own rowing. When an oarsman figures out what's going on, you encounter the problem of friends pulling harder for other friends. No one would ever admit to such a practice, but human nature would tell you differently.

Mike Spracklen had been around rowing long enough to know that seat racing was trouble. Over the years, he had developed his own selection methods, which turned out to be far tougher and more psychologically challenging than seat racing. Camp Spracklen-style meant rowing mostly in straight pairs (that is, without coxswains) and plenty of time trials. The pair is a lonely boat, which shows all too clearly who is effective and who is not. When you are out there with your partner, there is no one else to blame. The pair leaves nowhere to hide. For six weeks, we rowed most workouts in pairs, frequently switching partners to see who was quickest to adapt to a new situation.

The third day of camp, Spracklen called a meeting to explain the camp's training program and the philosophy behind it. Having trained under Mike for the past two months, some of us had already heard this speech. Little did we realize how often it would be repeated over the next four years. Spracklen's words were never magical, but they were effective in their clarity and simplicity. The following is a sample of what you would hear at the start of any training camp.

"We're going to talk for a minute about why we're here and what we're here to do. I have been hired to coach the men's eight. It is my goal for the eight to win a gold medal in Atlanta. Understand that in any situation I will give priority to the top guys, the guys who will be in that eight. If the eight wins a silver medal in Atlanta and the four wins gold, we have failed.

"As for selection of the eight, anyone who can row a pair well will certainly strengthen an eight. By switching partners at least every week, we'll see who is a consistent boat mover. Since we train in a pack, it will be clear who is always at the front. You don't have to go out and win every piece. What is more important is always being near the front and not being left miles behind. We'll hold a time trial every week or so to put the pressure on and see who is fastest. The time trial is when you need to worry about finishing first. In the weeks ahead, the work load will increase to prepare for upcoming races. Recognize now that you will have some good rows and some bad. Expect frustration, but more importantly learn to deal with it and gain from it. When you feel you can't go on another stroke, that is exactly the time to move forward."

In addition to a different style of training, Princeton was everyone's first experience with Spracklen's unique on-the-water coaching style. In most rowing programs, from high school to the national team, the coach rides alongside in his launch and barks out commands at his crews. Rowing has its fair share of quieter, brooding coaches, but most American coaches seem to be aggressive, hands-on types of managers. Even the greatest thinkers I have ever coxed for would scream at their crews on some occasion. No one has the same coolness and confidence as Spracklen exuded. When he was on the water, he was as relaxed as someone taking a stroll in the park. Amidst the violent storms on the water between pairs, Spracklen was like the lighthouse that you could count on for consistency.

While the rowers were busy getting used to their new training program, I was doing the same. Since they spent most practices in straight pairs, coxswains were virtually non-existent for a few weeks and I spent every session in the launch. I took this time to study Spracklen's coaching style, think about what to say in the boat and prepare for my own trials ahead.

While selection camp trudged onward, I found myself in a living environment that challenged me constantly. The majority of the squad stayed at the Princeton Ramada Inn on Route 1. Not having a clue what I was getting into, I moved into a triple with Mike Peterson and Will Porter, the self-proclaimed bad boys of the 1993 National Team.

Mike and Will were characters of the first variety. Both were excellent college oarsmen who had never quite made it at the next level. They had each won plenty of big races throughout their collegiate careers, but were often snubbed by national team coaches. Will had earned a silver medal at the 1991 Pan Am Games (the U.S. second team that year), while Mike had never earned a seat outside of college. But this was 1993, and everything was different. They were loud, fast, arrogant, and they let you know it all the time. Spracklen loved their enthusiasm, especially Peterson's boisterous, attacking style. Spracklen channeled their anger into pure fighting spirit as they assumed the bookends (stroke and bow) of the eventual 1993 national team eight.

On the water, they rowed their pair like a bat out of hell. It was ugly, unbalanced, and angry, but it was fast. Through years of pent-up frustration at previous failure, they had found a way to push each other beyond the limit. Hardly a practice went by when they rowed together that they didn't curse at someone on the lake. A lot of times they even yelled at each other. One day we received a note from a mother who's family lived on Carnegie Lake. She asked that we please consider the virgin ears of her young daughter before we shouted obscenities on the water. "Fuck that," Mike and Will responded.

Little did I know that off the water they would be just as difficult a tag team. They were both twenty-six years old and it seemed to me like they had done just about everything in life. Whether it was love life, travel, or business, they acted as though nothing could phase them. I, on the other hand, was the innocent young twenty-two year-old, who was putty in their hands. Those five weeks in room 602 of the Ramada

Hotel would be more of an adult education than a lot of people get in a lifetime.

Like the little brother they never had, Mike and Will put me through all the paces. First there were plenty of specific rules, violation of which invariably resulted in some form of physical punishment. Most important of these rules was the adherence to quiet time. Whether it was an afternoon nap or an early night's lights out I was under strict orders to not make a peep. I couldn't talk, I couldn't watch television, I couldn't listen to a walkman, and I couldn't type on my laptop computer. On several occasions, I was ordered to stop reading because I was turning the pages of a book too loudly!

The other area in which there were strict lines of distinction drawn was the sleeping arrangement. The room had two beds, one king size and one full-sized from a pull-out couch. Mike and Will switched between the two beds every week, while I slept with a sleeping bag on the floor in between the two of them. Looking back, I'm still not sure why I endured all this. After all I wasn't put in this room, I chose it on my own.

Despite these array of regulations, it was this living arrangement that began to teach me one of the most important lessons I would learn during my four years on the national team. There are lots of ways to build a fast crew—power, technique, or racing strategy to name a few. But one of the most elusive aspects of speed in the eight is the creation of the team chemistry. When you're forming an eight you are balancing ego-driven, mentally tough athletes and challenging them to work together as a unit. In other sports teamwork is important, but in rowing teamwork is essential. During their championship years, if the Chicago Bulls had an off night as a team, there was still a chance that Michael Jordan could have an outstanding individual performance and pull them through to victory. In a boat, if you don't pull together, you're not going to go anywhere.

There are also many ways to motivate a crew to go faster, and each of them works in their own right. Positive energy is far and away the most reliable tool. If you can learn to move a team forward by maintaining a positive attitude, then you're not just going to win the battle, you're going to win the war.

While Mike, Will, and I shared that room in Princeton I began to learn the importance of creating that foundation of positive teamwork. We would hang out in the room for hours on end chatting about stupid things. Although the discussions often bordered on the inane, there were just as many times when we talked about things close to the heart–hopes, dreams, and fears. This may not sound like the typical manly locker room banter you'd expect, but rowing is not a typical sport in that way.

My five weeks at the Ramada in Princeton were unforgettable. I experienced a period of true personal growth amidst the everyday pressures of selection. Like a military baptism by fire, my day to day tribulations made me that much tougher for what life had to offer.

America's collegiate phenom appeared nine days into selection camp. Jamie Koven arrived in Princeton fresh from a victory at the Royal Henley Regatta in England. Jamie had just finished his second year at Brown University, he had just turned twenty, and he was well on his way towards becoming America's rowing legend of the 1990s. In four years of high school rowing at St. Paul's School in New Hampshire he had lost two races. In two years at Brown he had yet to lose. He was the linchpin of the Brown varsity as a sophomore, and it looked like he would race for four years without ever losing.

No one really knew how to deal with Jamie at first. Most guys were out of college for a few years and had lost touch with the collegiate scene. But word got around in a hurry of Koven's winning streak, so his arrival made everyone on the starboard side that much more worried about another tough competitor. As time wore on, they would have plenty of reason to worry.

In high school and college, nearly all training is done in eights or fours. Since these are bigger boats they tend to be far more stable. Conversely, the pair is the most difficult boat to row technically because it is so unstable. Jamie and the other college oarsmen were at a disadvantage in training camp. Because they had little experience in the small boat, they faced more challenges than the veterans.

The difference between Jamie and other younger athletes was his ability to learn. Within a few weeks in a pair, Jamie was at the front of the pack. As final selection approached, Jamie had established himself as a core guy in Spracklen's eight. Once again, Koven had worked his magic. What Jamie displayed during those weeks in Princeton was the same work ethic that had carried him so far already. In addition to superior physiology, he was a good athlete and a good technical rower. There was nothing particularly outstanding when you looked at Jamie. But whenever you had any sort of competition you could count on him to be in the front. Jamie was the guy you passed the ball to for the final play of the game.

Nearly three weeks into camp, a new pair came to Princeton and requested a mini-trial of sorts to enter the athlete pool. Spracklen would not deny anyone a chance to compete for fear of a lawsuit in today's litigious society, so he allowed them to join our training for a few days. The pair included a couple of guys from Harvard, Bill Cooper and Chris Swan. They were both good guys, but coming from Harvard didn't really help. While Harvard has enjoyed the most illustrious reputation in the history of American collegiate rowing, the name wasn't worth a bucket of spit in our camp. Maybe it was jealousy, but this Harvard-less group generally thought the school produced one wacko after another. Chris and Bill were in store for some rough times.

During their first two days, the other pairs took a lot of pleasure in beating up on Chris and Bill. The Harvard pair saved face by not finishing last in every race, but they had worn out their welcome in Spracklen's eyes in a matter of forty-eight hours. At breakfast one morning we found this out rather clearly and in the process saw another side to our kindly British gentleman-coach.

Knowing Spracklen as I do now, I realize that everything he does is for an intended effect. Whether he is inspiring confidence or criticizing, there is always a larger lesson to be learned by the group, a sort of precedent. When Spracklen confronted Chris Swan at breakfast that morning in Princeton in front of the whole squad, we would all learn never to cross him.

Chris had asked Spracklen to come to Princeton for two days. Spracklen relented, but when those two days were up, Chris and Bill had not yet left. Mike wasted no time in making his feelings known publicly.

"Why are you still here, Chris?" Mike asked pointedly. Chris tried to stutter back a response, but to no avail. "You said you'd like to come for two days and now those days are up. You've shown you can't row with these guys. Why are you still here?"

Somehow Chris managed to stammer back an assertion that he belonged to be in the camp from the beginning. This prompted Mike to shoot back at him, "What have you done to deserve to be here? What have you won?"

"I was a member of the Olympic team," Chris responded confidently, in search of that Harvard charm.

"Oh," Mike said calmly, "what boat were you in?"

"Uh. I was a spare." Chris muttered.

"Well then, you weren't really in a boat. You weren't really on the Olympic team at all."

Chris responded with a history of how he had been a member of the Olympic sculling camp but then switched to sweep rowing to earn a spare spot in Barcelona at the last minute. Upon hearing this, Mike came back with the sharpest comment of all. "If you cannot scull, what makes you think that you can row at all?" Silence. By this point, all of us were beyond feeling badly for Chris. We were just hoping that he would make it out of there alive. But Spracklen's point had been made. He was in charge, and he would not tolerate someone waltzing in from outside to be a member of the training squad. Mike was running this show, and it was a one man act.

After weeks of training and knocking heads in pairs, the time had come for selection. Everyone thought they had their own read on how Spracklen would do it, but none of us could have imagined the chain of events that unfolded. Since the beginning of camp we had held time trials in the pairs. Boats would follow single file for a specified distance (usually 1500m or 2000m) in a race against the clock. By the end of July, as selection approached, Spracklen called for "an important time trial." The results from the trial would play a major role in selection. Once the trial was completed and results were announced, we all gathered in a meeting room in the Princeton boathouse.

Mike spoke briefly about selection to the group. His philosophy was that the gold medal was ours to win so we should choose ourselves. Mike would set the lead by choosing the first two athletes. Then, the group would grow larger and larger until the eight was filled out. Two seconds later, Mike asked Fred Honebein and Don Smith to go to another room with him. They were consistently the best oarsmen and guaranteed members of the eight. Now they would help select the next members of the crew.

Fifteen minutes later, Spracklen emerged and asked Jon Brown and Mike Peterson to join them. Now half of the seats in the eight were taken and nerves were becoming frayed. The wait for the next announcement was over half an hour. It seemed like days. Jamie Koven and Will Porter were asked to join the eight. By now Tom Murray was as angry as anyone in the room. He was the lone decliner not to be accepted in the eight and there was only one starboard seat left. This was it. Unfortunately the situation would not be resolved that day. When the coaches emerged from the selection room, they announced that the final two seats would be decided the next day. Five athletes were still in consideration and an on-the-water process would have to be used. The final port seat would go to Willie Castle or Jason Scott, while the final starboard seat would go to Scott Munn, Tom Murray or John Riley. Tom was devastated. I still did not know what the hell was going on.

The next morning we assembled for the final selection process. We hooked up the newest on-water speedometer to the eight and began testing. The six selected athletes would sit in their respective seats, while the five others would be rotated in for analysis. Each rotation would perform two twenty stroke pieces to get the boat up to maximum speed. The combination that produced the best score, according to the speedometer, would occupy the final two seats. As the day wore on, everyone felt the strain of the process. Coxing the boat that day, I was only too happy to see it end.

It was early afternoon when this grinding process finally came to an end. We had tried a variety of combinations, each of which necessitated a significant chunk of time in order to give each athlete his best possible opportunity. Heading into the last combination, the final port seat was awarded to Willie Castle. Meanwhile, the final starboard seat was up for grabs. In the next-to-last test, John Riley, an eight-time veteran of the national team, produced the highest score of the day. Spracklen called for one more shot for Tom Murray. Tom would get his two twenty-stroke chances and the better scoring starboard would occupy the boat's final seat.

As Tom's best friend, I found myself in an increasingly stressful situation. My best friend's rowing career was on the line and I would be the sole judge. The speedometer readout only appeared in my lap. While pacing the crew through their warm-up, you could feel the tension amongst the oarsmen. Five out of six decliners were in the crew, and the sixth's fate was on the line. You can bet that guys were prepared to pull as hard as possible for each twenty stroke piece.

The reason for two pieces was the wind. The wind was shifting throughout the day so we needed to do a piece of work in each direction of the river. A tail wind would push the boat faster than a head wind, so Tom truly only had one chance. His head wind score could never beat the best score of the day. It came down to one piece. I called for the boat to increase the power with my eyes transfixed on the LCD readout. With each stroke I could feel the rush of energy through the hull. As the boat got faster you could sense the ache of tired muscles. All the while the numbers on the screen climbed higher. His score crept closer and closer to John Riley's, and somewhere around stroke seventeen we broke the record. I shouted the results emphatically and the boat let out a cheer, not just of excitement, but of relief. The eight was picked. Tom was in.

Unfortunately, that did not mean that the coxswain of the eight was picked. Due to the emotional nature of athlete selection, the coxswain situation was swept under the rug. Spracklen finally announced a few days later that coxswain selection would take place the following week.

Monday July 26, 1993   *Princeton, NJ*

At this morning's meeting, we learned the plan for coxswain selection. Over the next two days Mikey Moore and I will switch in and out of the boat. Today's practices are mostly technical, while tomorrow they will be competitive. Tomorrow will be the true test. The U.S. lightweight eight will be here for race situations. I will take one workout and Mike the other. Assumedly, the crew will talk tomorrow and decide upon one cox.

There's nothing I can write that's going to help me through tomorrow. I've coxed plenty of boats through many tough practices and it's not going to be any different. What's done is done. I simply have to have faith that things will turn out in my favor.

The stress of this whole coxing situation got me pretty crazy before the weekend. I nearly lost it on Friday after worrying so much about my seat. When I finally found a bit of solitude, I had to fight off tears.

Rowing has been completely enjoyable for the last few months and I don't regret any decisions I have made. I'm sure that a few months from now I'll look back on this emotional slump and laugh as I enjoy the thrills that are still to come this season. I guess that what really hits me hard is the realization that I'm being drawn into competitive rowing so quickly that everything else is dropping off into the distance. It would be so easy to go back to a regular job in a regular apartment having a great time in life. I had a taste of that lifestyle and I enjoyed it thoroughly. But as I write, I feel the pressure of having to perform, to be judged, and to constantly prove my self-worth.

I understand that there are tremendous opportunities in front of me in various directions—athletics, employment, law school and so on. I am thankful that I'm so fortunate to have choices to make. Nevertheless, in times of intense pressure it is only natural to question your ability. What bothers me is that there looks to be no let-up of situations like this. Whether it's selection or world championship competition or merely the rigors of everyday practice, the pressure will always be on. Maybe I'm way off base here. Maybe life is a constant series of tough choices and daily strain. Maybe no matter which path I choose I will face difficulties. But nothing in my experiences has ever equaled the pressure of competing in the world of rowing. Consequently, surviving, and succeeding, in the rowing world provides fantastic preparation for anything else that life can throw at you.

Tuesday July 27, 1993   *Princeton, NJ*

Yeahhhhhhhhhh! This evening I was chosen as the cox for the 1993 United States Men's Heavyweight Eight for the World Championships in Prague, the Czech Republic. I only found out a little over an hour ago, but you can bet that I'm feeling on top of the world. I can't remember when I've been this psyched. The decision this evening signifies the end of a tremendously pressure-filled time period. Boy am I relieved.

I know there's plenty of pressure ahead for the summer, particularly to perform in the premier event at the World Championships. But for this moment I am in all my glory. There's actually nothing else to write. I'm so damned happy that I can't put any more on paper. This is bliss.

Immediately after cox selection, we drove to Canada to compete in the Royal Canadian Henley Regatta. This would be our only race preparation before the World Championships. It was not a highly competitive race, but we went for the experience. Regardless of who is on the line next to you, there is a certain build-up of pressure or stress. We wanted to go to St. Catherine's to experience some of those emotions.

The whole weekend was rather uneventful. We drove up, rowed on the course a few times, and then won by nearly ten seconds against below-average competition, an eternity in international competition. What I clearly remember is the reaction of the crowds while we received our medals. St. Catherine's is just across the U.S. border, so there were plenty of American fans in attendance. As we pulled into the victory dock the crowd started cheering, "USA! USA! USA!" I remember thinking, "Don't these people know that this race wasn't that big a deal? What are they all excited about?"

They were excited about seeing the American National Team in action. It had not dawned on me until that moment that I was there as a representative of the United States. The fact snuck up on me all of the sudden and made me as nervous as it did proud. For the next two months, I was no longer racing for myself. I was racing for my country.

Immediately after the Canadian Henley, we set up camp at Dartmouth College in Hanover, New Hampshire. This camp was designed to be our final testing ground before departing for the upcoming World Championships in Prague. In mid-August, Dartmouth is an ideal training site. The Connecticut River is a long, windy stretch of water that allows you to row for miles in any direction. The weather is comfortable, the food is good and the university is friendly. It is no surprise that national team squads had been going to Dartmouth for decades.

We spent only twelve days in Dartmouth, but it seemed closer to twelve months. The limitless water allowed Spracky to row the guys into the ground. We would need all the hard training we could get because time had now become a factor. Once we left for the World Championships, jet lag would severely affect our training schedule. Virtually all work in Europe would be a taper in preparation for the regatta. Dartmouth was the final and most important preparation stage of the summer.

While the guys rowed themselves closer to death three times per day, I was fighting my own demons of weight loss. As the days wore on in Dartmouth my obsession grew more intense. Today, I can look back and realize that I had developed a full-fledged eating disorder. The dieting I endured for four years still affects me today. I still become full after eating a small meal, and I can't gain an ounce above 125 pounds no matter what I eat.

I started out by cutting back on eating—less meat, more salad, non-fat milk, and so on. That was enough to get me down around 120 pounds, but I still had to lose ten pounds—more than 8% of my body weight. Each day I took another precaution in order to drop the weight. Throughout the summer I could rationalize procrastinating my diet slightly. Now it was mid-August and the World Championships were right around the corner. I had to do it now or not do it at all. Besides, the guys were sacrificing their bodies. Why couldn't I sacrifice mine?

I was running at least an hour once each day, sometimes twice a day. I ate virtually nothing once the sun set, chewed tobacco for dinner and chugged Diet Cokes to keep my stomach full. Worst of all, though, was the addiction I developed to laxatives. I couldn't bring myself to stick my finger down my throat, so laxatives seemed to be the next best thing. By the time we reached the World Championships, I was gobbling several tablets each day and wrenching my intestines. The only positive aspect of this horrible experience is that it has allowed me to truly understand the trauma many young women go through with anorexia or bulimia. Throughout the summer I knew what it was like to obsess about food and weight.

Sunday August 15, 1993   *Hanover, NH*

I went on two runs today to try to drop weight, the first for forty-five minutes, and the second for an hour. Unfortunately, the weight just doesn't seem to be coming off as I had hoped. My overall plan was to be a comfortable 115 pounds by the flight to Prague in six days. That goal was coming along just fine. By the middle of last week I was down to 115.5. But then, for reasons I don't comprehend, I went up beyond 117 and I haven't been able to bring it down again, not even to 116.9. The only thing I can figure is that this dining hall food is killing me somehow. I'm pretty careful about what I eat, trying to limit myself to only two meals per day. Even at those meals I don't eat that much. Nevertheless, I find myself maintaining a weight around 117.

There's no way around it. I have to lose approximately seven pounds in the next two to three weeks in order to give my boat the best chance in the World Championships. Losing that weight drives me right up a wall! The guys in the boat are actually very cool about my situation. They don't give me a hard time about what I eat. They recognize that I'm doing my best, and I figure they just assume I'll do my job and make weight.

The clear problem is that we're now in the final stages of preparation for the biggest race of all of our lives. Each of us has rowed for more than five or ten years to get to this moment, and we all want to do our absolute best. I cannot afford to let this losing weight bullshit affect the way I approach competition. That particularly includes my attitude around the guys. I have to deal with my weight loss in a professional manner that does not affect my performance as a member of the crew.

Yes, the first step is recognition of the problem, and I don't think it's taken me long to recognize it. I've known it all along. The next step is to solve the problem, to be above the rigors of weight loss. In this case there's really no way around it. I've got to deal with it from now through September 5th. If I hope to continue my career on the national team, I'm going to have to do this again and again, right up until one beautiful day in the summer of 1996 in Atlanta. I have to realize that weight loss will make every day a bitch, but I've got to overcome it.

I wish there were some trick, some way to get this monkey off my back. But I know there is no easy way. The only real way is to be as strong as possible, to think strong thoughts, and to rise to greatness. I've had to struggle with the issue of weight loss throughout my wrestling career, and it's not too different now except that (1) the stakes are much higher; and (2) I have to deal with more than just myself. In wrestling I was the whole team because it's an individual sport. Today I am part of a crew–nine different people who must work to together towards one goal. I don't want to let them down. I must remain confident that fate will guide me through this process, and that in the end it will all fall into place.

The great irony here is that I've been coxing for nearly a decade, and today I stand upon the threshold of the greatest opportunity of my career. Yet I can't wait for the race to be over so that I can return to a "normal" life. I'm sure the rowers often feel the same way. Coach has put them through training hell this summer and they, too, want to win this race, get it over with and enjoy the benefits of victory. For all of us the challenge is to remain focused on the difficult task at hand without looking forward so much to the day it's over. The funny thing is that I'll bet that once the race is over we'll all yearn for the days when we trained our nuts off to get to that point. Victory or not, we'll all look back and say, "Boy, I wish I had taken the time to smell the roses in Dartmouth." I don't want to do that. I want to leave the dock in Prague with my head high knowing that I always gave the boat every ounce of energy and determination I had. I want to look back with a sense of pride.

I am reminded of my favorite quote from **The Power of One** by Bryce Courtenay:

> "The power of one is above all things the power to believe in yourself, often well beyond any latent ability you may have previously demonstrated. The mind is the athlete; the body is simply the means it uses to run faster or longer, jump higher, shoot straighter, kick better, swim harder, hit further, or box better. [My friend's] dictum to me, 'First with the head and then with the heart,' was more than simply mixing brains with guts. It meant thinking well beyond the powers of normal concentration and then daring your courage to follow your thoughts."

I know my goals: win a World Championship, and at the same time reach 110 pounds. It's now time to see just how much courage I really possess. Three weeks from today, we'll have completed our season. I have three weeks to learn a great deal about my courage.

The 1993 U.S. Eight in Hanover. From left to right:
Tom Murray, Willie Castle, Will Porter, Jon Brown, Steven Segaloff, Jamie
Koven, Don Smith, Mike Peterson (kneeling), and Fred Honebein.

Saturday August 21, 1993   **NYC–Prague**

*It's fair to say that I've coxed for eight plus years to get to this point. I
am aboard a plane-full of American rowers en route to the World
Championships to represent our country. Even better, I'm part of the premier boat, one with the ability to win it all.*

*We'll eventually arrive in Prague sometime Sunday afternoon local
time to begin the final training process. Our first race is scheduled for
Tuesday August 31st, and depending on how many entries there are we
could race several times throughout the week. The championship final for
the men's eight will be the last race of the whole regatta, sometime around
5pm on Sunday September 5th.*

The 1993 World Championships were held in Racice, a small paper-
mill town one hour outside of Prague in the Czech Republic. We spent one
week training and the second week racing. For two weeks we experienced

exactly what you would expect in Eastern Europe–cold, rain, and darkness. Amidst this dreary backdrop our crew would be battle tested. We arrived in the Czech Republic international novices and left hungry warriors. Unfortunately, like most of life's best lessons, we learned the hard way.

Friday August 27th, 1993   *Racice, Czech Republic*

Things are a little tense amongst the group lately. Thus far, one of this boat's greatest assets has been its good-natured attitude. We have nine guys who get along quite well and enjoy going fast. Up to this point, we really haven't felt any pressure.

Yesterday we participated in a 2000m time trial with many other American boats. Our performance was sub-standard–5 minutes 38 seconds. Since hearing the results of that piece everyone has gotten their shorts in a bundle. There was a headwind and the piece was a bit flat, plus we all know that 5.38 isn't going to get you jack shit next weekend. So all of the sudden, guys are starting to get on each other's nerves. In addition to the time trial performance, our tension is directly related to a variety of other factors, including staying in a depressing mill town in Eastern Europe; dealing with the fatigue of jet-lag; the burden of performing in a World Championship for the first time in a highly touted crew; and simply the trickiness of getting up and down a crowded course.

Specifically, there was a confrontation between a few members of the crew after the time trial. One guy made a few comments in front of everyone that he never should have said. In essence, this individual openly questioned the ability of some other boat members to perform. The comment infuriated the rest of the crew and formed a rift that would take a few years to heal.

We need to stay positive. The next week and three days represent the greatest rowing opportunity in all of our careers. We have the chance to carve our names forever in U.S. rowing history, and we shouldn't let one practice get to us. Now is the time to prove just how tough we really are.

Personally, I'm trying my damnedest to shrug off the fatigue of severe weight loss (including two runs per day) and rise to the occasion of leading this crew to victory. Spracky talked to us this morning and provided some insightful comments. He told us that we were a bit too arrogant going into yesterday's piece, or this whole regatta, for that matter. He said that we need to better understand the enormity of commitment it's going to take to win a medal next weekend. To beat any one of the Aussies, the Dutch, the Germans and the Romanians will take tremendous execution. To beat all of them will take the performance of our lives.

Right now, we need to sit back and re-focus our energy on pure performance. We are capable of succeeding in this endeavor, but we need to be at our best. In the upcoming days, it's my job to liven these guys up, to make sure we always feel like we're moving forward in a very positive way. In ten years I won't remember the rigor of weight loss, but I sure as hell will remember the result of next weekend's final. I don't want to look back and ask myself, "What if?"

Monday August 30th, 1993   **Racice, Czech Republic**

Race day has nearly arrived. The World Championships officially opened yesterday. We start racing tomorrow and I'm pumped for a big one. In the first heat are Netherlands, Romania, Russia, Lithuania and Poland. We are in the second heat with Germany, Australia, Great Britain and the Czech Republic, where only the winner advances to the final. The crew to beat is definitely the Germans, but we also expect the Aussies to get out fast and try to hold on.

After our boat meeting, it's clear that our game plan is to approach this as a time trial by focusing on our own race strategy and not get caught up in a what the other boats are doing. We expect the Aussies to blast out of the gate; on the other hand, the Germans should be strong off the line with a monster move somewhere in the middle 1000m. As always, we're looking to get out fast, hold an aggressive pace through the middle, and lift to the line. We certainly have the potential to win this thing tomorrow, but it will take a great effort.

Personally, I'm really not that nervous. Sure this is the World Championships, but at the same time, it's just another regatta and I'm here to win. I think it's critical that I stay relaxed to keep the crew calm. All we can do is give it our best effort. Nothing more, nothing less.

My weight is pretty good, 112 pounds this morning, and I'm hopeful I'll reach 110 pounds for Sunday. Although I'm pretty tired nowadays, and certainly ready to eat my brains out.

Spracklen had a good psychological read on our crew for our heat. He could sense the increased pressure, so he worked to keep us calm and focused. We had talked about the specifics of our race plan and discussed the importance of perfect execution. But in those moments before a World Championship race, you don't always need a rah-rah speech.

When we gathered just before launching for the 1993 World Championship heat, Spracklen spent some of the time joking around. First he made sure that we were all on the same page strategically and we knew exactly what we wanted to accomplish. Then his speech deviated from an intense tone towards one of humor. We had been playing around that week with a walkie-talkie system that allowed Mike to speak to our crew from the shore. During major regattas coaches cannot use motor boats, so they are restricted to biking alongside and yelling. Mike's closing remarks that afternoon in the Czech Republic were, "Oh yes. Do go out and win because then we can use the free days to experiment with the walkie-talkies." His timely humor peeled away an unneeded layer of tension.

Tuesday August 31, 1993   ***Racice, Czech Republic***

Unbelievable. We just beat the Germans by nearly three seconds and we weren't even pushed. The best part is that it wasn't a particularly amazing race. Sure we had a very solid piece, and we all committed to attacking the race plan. There is no doubt in any of our minds that we can reproduce that sucker on Sunday in the race that counts.

I can't say that I was totally surprised. Indeed, I thought we would win. But to drive through them so fluidly was incredible. Before we knew it, we hit the 1250m and there was no doubt we were gonna rock 'em.

Coming into the last 500m, the only thing I was thinking was no mistakes. In the end, we bettered the German eight by 2.87 seconds, and we all felt great. In the other heat, the Romanians beat the Dutch by two to three seconds in a time over two seconds slower than ours.

Right now, almost six hours after the race, I'm only starting to come out of the fog. Ever since we hit the dock I have been pinching myself, wondering, "How fast are we?" Three seconds is an eternity in the men's eight. We can do that again. The trick now is to keep things sharp, remain aggressive and stay focused. The final could be a totally different story. I don't think for a second the Germans aren't going to come up with something new for Sunday, or the Romanians or the Dutch for that matter.

With the intensity of the week constantly rising, we were given one afternoon off to relax. Some guys spent the day touring Prague, while others hung out with visiting girlfriends. I chose a completely different path. My parents had come to watch the racing, and they suggested a visit to a nearby concentration camp, Terezin. I had never seen a concentration camp, and as a Jew I felt it would be a tremendous learning experience. I must have been quite a sight that day.

I looked thin enough to occupy a cell in the awful place at 110 pounds. We walked around the grounds observing the remnants of a horrible past. I felt nothing but emptiness. It struck me as sickening to think that within twenty minutes of the sight of my rowing dreams was a small area of land that had served as a killing ground for so many. The camp had all the makings of a horror movie–gas chambers, ovens, and thousands of graves. My visit there had no relation to my emotions going into the final day of competition, but it did serve to remind me that life offered far worse tragedies than not winning a World Championship.

Friday September 3, 1993   *Racice, Czech Republic*

It's now the night before the night before. I'm ready to go. Truthfully, the boat could use another day of paddling. We had a rather average practice today, probably because we're all a bit anxious to get it on. It's been three days since our race. Virtually all of the thrill of that victory is gone. The heat gave us plenty of confidence, but we all know the final is going to be a different story. Mike still says the Germans are the crew to beat, and you can bet they're gonna be ready for us. As much as I'm ready to race, not to mention end this diet, it will be helpful to watch a day of finals tomorrow to see the atmosphere and be ready for Sunday's antics. It's still just another race.

Saturday September 4, 1993   *Racice, Czech Republic*

It's 8am. I just showered after my daily morning trot to the race course and back. I was sitting in the tub thinking about tomorrow's race and it hit me that this is easily the biggest race of my life. But what struck me as funny was the fact that I've made the same comment, "this race is the biggest in my life," several times already this summer. I can specifically point to at least three instances: Duisburg, Indianapolis, and coxswain selection. My point is that tomorrow is the biggest race of my life. But at the same time there is nothing I can do differently to be better prepared.

I guess it comes back to something Spracky told me in Dartmouth. We were riding in the launch one afternoon and I asked him, "What do I have to do in the coming weeks in order to win the World Championship?" He turned away for a moment, then looked back and said, "Do your best." The bottom line is that you can't do more than your best because that's all there is.

The 1993 U.S. Eight in Racice. From left to right: Will Porter, Jamie Koven, Willie Castle, Tom Murray, Steven Segaloff, Jon Brown, Don Smith, Fred Honebein and Mike Peterson.

Sunday September 5, 1993   **Racice, Czech Republic**

Race day has finally arrived. Since gathering in Rutgers back in early May, we've been focused towards this day and now it's here. From a personal perspective I have been coxing for nearly ten years to get to this point–the most important eight race of the year.

It's now 2:20pm, and we're hanging around the hotel making last minute preparations for the 3pm bus that will take us to the course. As soon as we arrive I need to weigh-in. I have been eating today to get UP to 110 pounds. Launch time is around 4:10pm and start time is 5pm.

I feel quite good. I'm naturally a bit nervous, but on the whole, I'm trying to soak up the whole atmosphere. It's been a long road here, and I'm determined to enjoy the day.

We had a practice already today, a race warm-up at lunch time, which went quite well. We nailed our power pieces and that give me the all-important confidence to know that we're going to come of the line blasting and give this our best shot. That's all we can do. No magic tricks, no special karma. What we're gonna do is execute and perform to the best of our abilities.

When race time finally arrived our levels of anxiety had gone off the charts. It had been five days since our first race in the regatta. For some reason, the rest of the American team had decided that we would win. This constant stream of assumption ended up hurting more than helping. Our supporters are not to blame in any way, however the constant reaffirmation of our abilities caused a build-up of over-confidence that was fatal. Without the scars of battle experience, we were not quite ready to win the big one. We could jump out to a lead and hold on, but we could not race from behind to win.

Monday September 6, 1993   **Racice, Czech Republic**

Our race is in the history books. The Germans won, 2.25 seconds ahead of the Romanians, who were 1.75 seconds ahead of us. Australia followed in fourth, Netherlands in fifth, and Great Britain in sixth. I'm experiencing a variety of emotions, which run the gamut of anger at not winning to pride at our results. It's nearly 2am, but I want to express my feelings while today's memory is fresh.

A quick description of the race. We got out of the blocks pretty well in terms of pure speed, only 0.2 seconds behind Romania at 500m and in second place. However, and we knew this would be the key, we simply did not establish the rhythm necessary to pull off the victory. As expected, the Germans pounded out the middle 1000m and that's where they earned the victory. We tried on numerous occasions to resurrect the rhythm but it just wasn't meant to be. The Germans continued to march throughout the race and pull away from the field. The Romanians inched ahead of us, and we couldn't nose ahead of them for the silver. At the finish line, the Australians sprinted hard, but we withheld their charge to capture the bronze.

After the thrill of the World Championships, a group of us had decided to take advantage of being in Europe by spending an extra two weeks traveling. We bought Eurail tickets and planned our itinerary on the go. Already in Prague, we decided to spend a few days there and then explore some of Eastern Europe's newly opened capital cities. After two days in Prague, we boarded an overnight train for Budapest, Hungary. This first train ride would prove to be quite eventful.

Two of the biggest guys on the U.S. team were in our group, Don Smith at 6'8" and Duncan Kennedy at 6'9". They shared a train compartment that evening through the Eastern European countryside. Stretched out along the seats, they slept through the evening as the train rambled through foreign lands. By dawn, we raced through Bratislava when Don knocked on my compartment and entered in a flurry of activity.

"Did you guys take my fanny pack? You know, as a joke."

"No." I answered and shook my head.

"Well," Don said. "It's pretty much gone, and I don't know where it is. It's got my passport and everything else in it. The conductor needs to see it now."

"Are you sure you checked your compartment?" Fred asked. Both of us were on the verge of laughter, but wary of Don's temper.

"Well, I'll go check again I guess. Fuck!" Don said angrily. By now he was not just frustrated, but worried also.

He spilled out his train car, but still came up empty. The conductor spoke little English, but he made it clear that Don had to leave the train immediately. Suddenly, our little journey around Eastern Europe had turned into a messy situation. At the next stop a few minutes later, I gave Don $100 cash and said good-bye in the middle of Bratislava. We agreed to meet up through the American Express office in Budapest as soon as possible.

Don made it through the situation. Barely. The $100 was just enough to buy a new passport at the American consulate in Bratislava, a sausage to fill his stomach, and a ticket to Budapest. Amazingly, we all met randomly two days later in the bathroom of our hostel in Hungary.

After a few more days of traveling throughout Europe, our group headed back to the United States. Spracky didn't circulate an official training program, and we were left alone for a few months. There would be plenty of time to train as a squad since the team would be officially centered in San Diego, California at the start of 1994. The U.S. Olympic Committee was building the first Olympic Training Center in warm weather in Chula Vista, California, twenty minutes south of downtown San Diego, and our squad was going to be the first official residents of the center. We would soon find out that perhaps we had arrived in San Diego a little ahead of schedule.

Chapter 2: 1994

It is only fitting that the 1994 season began in difficult and uncomfortable conditions. We were forced to band together as a unit and work hard for every inch of ground. There is no doubt in my mind that the obstacles we overcame in those early months built an inner toughness that made us unbeatable when we encountered outside competition. We pulled together as a team and pulled for each other to win every race.

When we arrived in San Diego just after the first of the year, it was hard to find the ARCO Olympic Training Center that lured us to California. There was a large plot of land in the desert where dozens of landscapers worked feverishly each day, but that was about it. Construction had barely begun, and the myth of a training center with a huge new boathouse, dining facilities and athlete housing was filled only with horticulture. There may not have been anywhere to eat or sleep, but the site had one hell of a garden.

The other noticeable feature of the future Olympic Training Center was its proximity to the Mexican border. The most popular vehicles on the road in the area were U.S. Border Patrol cars. Later in the season, we caused a huge ruckus when we registered at the prestigious Henley Royal Regatta under the club name "Border Patrol Boat Club" with matching uniforms. The powers that be in USRowing were mortified and they demanded that we change our outfits.

USRowing had established a connection to the Navy, so our squad was granted permission to live in the Bachelors Officers Quarters (BOQ) at the 32nd Street Naval Station in National City for $9 per day. The base was twenty minutes south of downtown San Diego and twenty minutes east of the training center by highway. The rooms were nice enough, but we would soon learn that the Navy had plenty of rules about keeping them in order.

During those initial months in San Diego, our training schedule was strict. We would get two full days off, the only time that would happen in the next three years, but they would be earned. The other five days of the week, most of our time would be spent on the water or en route to the boathouse. Due to logistics, we would train two times per day in long sessions rather than three shorter sessions. The "boathouse" was a shipping container stuck at the end of a parking lot that abutted the lake. Because there were no facilities, except for two Port-o-lets, we did not have anywhere to wait around in between training except in our cars. We had to return to the naval base. The commute from the naval base to the boathouse was a solid half-hour, which meant at least two hours each day on the road.

This training schedule gave us virtually no time to work. With no income, but everyday living expenses, people definitely felt strapped for money. The only salvation was the minimal grant ($5000) that some of us received for the year from the U.S. Olympic Committee. Wallets were tight.

During that first month Spracklen admonished us to put our situation in perspective. At one of our earliest team meetings he said, "I just want to talk about the job situation for a minute. If you want to succeed at something, at anything, it's a measure of your determination. How much time, how much training you put into that effort will produce a certain level of success. Ideally, you want to be there for every session, every practice. But it is your decision. I am just the coach of this team. You are the athletes. It is your gold medal to win or lose. I can only tell you what I know from experience. We all came out here to be the best in the world. It's your own personal decision to look for part-time jobs. After finishing third last summer, we know we're not quite good enough yet. We can hardly afford to take the time off." There was no doubt where Spracklen stood. We would train, not work.

Tuesday January 11, 1994   *San Diego, CA*

We finally arrived here at the Naval Base. After a lengthy check-in process, I am writing from my new home in Copp Hall, Bachelor's Officers Quarters. Each of these rooms is set up the same way. There's one common room with a few couches and a microwave. Four single rooms surround the common area. Each single is nicely furnished with a queen size bed, nightstand with lamp, desk, mirror, television and VCR, two dressers, three good-sized closets, a refrigerator and a bathroom with a shower.

The time has come to put up or shut up. The rowers have just begun practice five days a week (Wednesdays and Saturdays off), and months of physical torture. We have talked about training together full-time as a group since my first day at Rutgers back in May. Now it is reality. It's hard to believe.

I have the opportunity to train for the U.S. National Rowing Team, and hopefully the U.S. Olympic Team on the brink of tremendous success. This core group of guys has risked everything to move out here and pursue a dream. I can never lose sight of the fact that every ounce of sweat and energy is devoted towards that shining day in Atlanta more than two years away.

Throughout college I enjoyed jogging for fitness sake. In my first season on the national team I began running seriously to help drop the extra weight. In San Diego, I developed a love for running. In the years to come, running would become an integral part of my development as a coxswain. Getting out on the road by myself for hours every week made me mentally and physically sharp.

Only two weeks after my arrival in San Diego, I found the first out- ·
let for my new found running passion, the San Diego Marathon.

Saturday January 22, 1994   **San Diego, CA**

Tomorrow, I'm set to run my first marathon. I can remember thinking about running a marathon since my junior year at Cornell in 1990, and now I'll get my chance. I'm not in prime shape, but I refuse to ignore this opportunity. Regardless of anything that happens, I have to convince myself that above all else I'm crossing that damned finish line. Tomorrow is all about conquering the self.

The thing I'm most excited about tomorrow is the toughness of the distance. People say that you undergo some tremendous changes any time before or around that twenty-mile mark, the wall. I want to go to the wall and beyond. I want to be able to look deep within and see what's there. And then I want to do it again and again in other marathons.

Sunday January 23, 1994   **Carlsbad, CA**

Sitting alone on a curb after just finishing the San Diego Marathon, I need to write in my journal to reflect upon the immediacy of such a monumental event. It is around noon, and over an hour ago I crossed the line in my first, and certainly not last, marathon.

Today represents the achievement of a five-year dream. I ran faster than I imagined: 3 hours, 26 minutes, and 26 seconds, which is less than eight minutes per mile. I can't even begin to describe the elation I felt. It wasn't "runner's high," but it was an incredible surge. From mile fifteen through twenty-five, I relished the signals of pain from my body, wanting to savor every jolt. At mile twenty I expected to be in a small, dark tunnel, "the wall," but it never really happened. Miles twenty-three and twenty-four were very difficult, but the sign at mile marker twenty-five provided untold inspiration. My mind took over my body. I ignored the agony and increased the pace. In the final mile, a relay team member pushed up and kept me fired up for the final stretch. After the sign for twenty-six I didn't think, I just went. Before I knew it, I was sprinting the home stretch cheering to myself, "Here we go!" repeatedly. As I crossed the line, a desire overtook me to shake a fist in the air celebrating the finish. Instead, I simply felt a wave of happiness, of accomplishment, of finality.

Now to find another marathon.

Monday January 24, 1994   San Diego, CA

I have plenty of reflections upon yesterday's momentous occasion, but observation number one has to be the most obvious, PAIN. You don't really think about how much it's going to hurt afterwards, but it's not incidental. My legs are killing me. Last evening, despite being completely wiped out, I could not sleep. I've been icing all day and taking painkillers, but the soreness isn't going away. It will probably take four to five days before things will feel fully functional. Still, the pain is 100% worth it.

After thinking about the past thirty-six hours, I have come to view yesterday as much more than a race, and closer to a spiritual experience. Running the marathon presented a new type of challenge. Instead of worrying about finishing time or being competitive, I simply ran my race. The only challenge, and it wasn't a small one, was to complete the distance. The marathon was great because of its paradoxical challenge. I didn't feel the types of pressure associated with a big crew race because there were no expectations. But at the same time, I wondered if my body and mind were capable of performing such a feat.

This latter part of the challenge, the challenge of self, allowed me to put everything else out of my head. I had plenty of peripheral thoughts, but they all paled in comparison to the ringing chorus of "Just finish the race." I found a new philosophy of thought, one that chose to laser beam focus on the present, the immediate present. Any event before that moment became an unimportant thought, a wasted thought, and a thought that did not matter. Even at mile ten, mile nine became obsolete. All that mattered was the next step, the next mile.

Yesterday taught me the valor in giving your best effort. When you set out to accomplish something, do your best. Put your body, your mind, and your very existence on the line and see what happens. If you can maintain your focus and your strength, you will accomplish your goal. But the only way to find out is to try your best.

Our first few months in San Diego were relatively uneventful. There were nearly twenty oarsmen training, but less than half of this original group would make any National Team boat. Since Spracklen had opened the camp to any interested oarsmen, he attracted a wide variety of talent. A number of athletes who had never made the grade came to San Diego in search of a dream that would never become reality. As for the established national team from the year before, results were mixed.

When we began in the early months of January, only four guys from the eight came (JB, Fred Honebein, Tom Murray and Don Smith), and none from the next priority boat, the straight four. January 1994 was simply too far away from the Olympics in July of 1996. In Olympic rowing history, the U.S. squad had not trained year-round in a structured program in any year other than the Olympic year. When Spracklen announced that his plan called for full-time training in January of 1994, his philosophy was not warmly received. Some athletes did not hesitate to move to San Diego and follow anything that Spracklen said. Others continued jobs or school on the east coast, trained in their own time, and waited until the season crept closer before moving west.

In time, Spracklen began to draw more talent to his squad. In February, Chip McKibben, a four-time national team sculler from Newport Beach, came down to train for a day. One of our athletes was sick, so Chip filled in one of the pairs for an afternoon. Chip's boat went very well and he was immediately lured to move to San Diego. Chip had experienced moderate success in sculling, but his time was running out. Chip was fast approaching thirty and desperately in search of a World Championship. In addition to his experience, Chip McKibben brought a good-natured attitude to the squad. He always had a big smile, and frequently lightened up a tense situation.

In early April, another two proven oarsmen joined Spracklen's camp, Sean Hall and Jeff Klepacki. Both guys had been on many national teams and were members of the bronze medal straight four in Prague. After five World Championships, they had finally earned their first medal. Now they came to San Diego to win the gold medal. Training at home throughout the winter, they arrived in San Diego figuring they were in pretty good shape. Wrong. There is virtually no way any oarsman can walk into the Spracklen's training system and be ready for it. The rigors of training in pairs several times per day is a load that puts enormous pressure, both physical and mental, on the athlete. Jeff and Sean would get beat up for a month or so, but Spracklen recognized their potential. Here were two talented, powerful athletes, who could make an immediate impact in his eight.

Monday April 18, 1994   *National City, CA*

Rowers often discuss how the lessons they learn through intensive training provide them with a blueprint for success in other endeavors. The lessons they have learned from rowing teach life-long lessons about success, for example, the merits of hard work, the necessity of teamwork, the power to focus on a single goal, and so on. Each individual athlete must fight daily battles to prove his worth, and in the process learn about how to win those battles.

Whether you're talking about elite rowers here in San Diego, women's rowers in Chattanooga, lugers in Lake Placid, wrestlers in Colorado Springs, volleyballers in San Diego, or any other Olympic hopeful, you're dealing with an elite athletic mind. Every minute, every piece, every day, every week and every season you have to question if it's worth it. Will you even make it to the glory of competition in Atlanta in three years? And even if you do make it, will it be worthwhile? Obviously, those who have made such enormous sacrifices think it's worth it; otherwise they wouldn't devote such a chunk of their life.

What I'm proposing is that the final destination for athletes is not as praiseworthy compared to the arduous path they must traverse in order to reach the moment of glory. *That is the essence of the challenge. Olympic hopefuls fight every battle to the death, as if it were their last. They persevere through highs and lows in search of a few minutes of magnificence.*

The U.S. Olympic contingent marches into the giant stadium, only to hear the deafening roar of the crowd. The cameras are rolling, the fans are cheering exuberantly, and televisions around the nation are tuned into this remarkable Opening Ceremony. America's best athletes revel in the brief spotlight, enjoying the fruits of untold years of labor. Days later, after a winning performance, the Olympic Champion climbs to the top of the podium to accept the gold medal. Tears stream down his face as his nation's anthem is played and his flag is raised for all to see. The hours of training, the ups and downs of previous competition are forgotten during one of the most poignant moments in modern sport.

For thousands of Olympic hopefuls, that moment is what pushes them through innumerable hours of training. That moment represents the answer to the daily question, is it all worth it? Today, I am one of those Olympic hopefuls. I am one who uses that dream as the answer to any questions of self-doubt. In these days of multi-million dollar contract negotiations and major sponsor endorsements, the thousands of American athletes who devote their entire life to the Olympic Dream in less popular sports are often forgotten. America should honor the select few who make the enormous leap on top of the podium, for they are the absolute best of the best. However, America should also do more to recognize the thousands of others who battle constantly to reach that point.

The elite athlete, one who can even reach the level of realistically training for the Olympics, is a unique breed in itself. In his journey, there are unmistakable lessons learned along the way, more than could be listed on any simple piece of paper. During this pilgrimage you learn what it takes to put your best abilities on the line every day. You learn about the value of hard work, pushing well beyond the limits your mind has previously set. You learn lessons of triumph and tragedy, self-confidence and self-doubt. Moreover, these lessons are by no means fleeting, but rather life enhancing. They are the bricks that form the core of an individual. In the process, the athlete doesn't merely learn about success, he becomes success.

This spewing forth of emotion on paper has been prompted by my own excitement to get into racing season. Duisburg is now less than five weeks away, and it's time for me to start focusing intensely on the work that lays ahead. As the season's start draws near, I have to begin to shut everything out except the main focus of this entire process, a World Championship. I can't close off everyone and everything else around me because it's not healthy. But in order to win a world championship during the five and a half minutes on September 18th, 1994 I must have done it in my mind a million times.

Last summer taught me many things about race day preparation, and I continue to learn with every practice and every race. But my concentration must become more focused, like a laser beam pointed at a distant point. For me, focus begins with weight loss. I need to eat less and exercise more to hone my mental skills. I need to push my body beyond its own limits into a world where all that matters is the unity of the boat and the performance of the crew.

We began the 1994 racing season with a two week trip to Germany. The eight selected for this competition was rough and ready. Because collegiate rowing season was not yet over and some of last year's team had not yet moved to San Diego, this eight contained a mix of characters. Additionally, Don Smith injured his back, so we missed his presence in the boat. The crew included three guys from the 1993 U.S. eight, Jon Brown, Fred Honebein, and Tom Murray; three guys with lots of other national team experience, Sean Hall, Jeff Klepacki, and Chip McKibben; and two brothers who had been around national camps for a long time, Jerome and Tim Ryan. This eight proved that a big heart could make a big difference.

Wednesday May 11, 1994   *San Diego–Frankfurt*

Our plane is scheduled to land within the next forty-five minutes for the first leg of our trip to Germany, a trip that officially commences the 1994 racing season. Practice has been going very well the past few weeks, and the eight is moving surprisingly fast. It is hard to believe that the battle is about to begin. We have been training and have not raced in what seems like eons. It is strange to think of starting up again at all. I probably feel this more than the guys because I'm not on the water fighting it out every day as they do.

Of course, my biggest concern right now is weight. What else is new? Tom, Fred and other guys have specifically told me not to worry about it at all. But I have to deal with it as best possible by dropping as many pounds without sacrificing an ounce of mental sharpness. In an effort to admit my continuing eating disorder, I am sad to note that starting tomorrow Ex-Lax will become an integral part of my daily diet.

We planned to row in two different regattas while in Germany. Shortly after arrival, we competed in a tune-up race in Mannheim to shake out the cobwebs. The following weekend at Duisburg would be the focus of the trip. In Mannheim, we struggled to shrug off the effects of nine hours of jet lag and did okay. On the first day of the regatta, we won our final against mediocre competition. In the second day, a formidable Romanian crew led from start to finish to beat us by two and a half seconds.

Given an additional week to prepare for Duisburg and adjust to the significant time change, our crew grew excited about our opportunity. Under Spracky's psychological tutelage, we approached Duisburg as a no-lose situation. We considered ourselves a throw-together crew facing the best the world had to offer. If we could give the competition a run for their money, who knew what we would be capable of with a full arsenal?

Heinous uniforms, but a gutsy crew at the 1994 Duisburg Regatta. From left to right: Chip McKibben, Fred Honebein, Sean Hall, Jon Brown, Mike Spracklen, Tom Murray, Steven Segaloff, Jeff Klepacki, Jerome Ryan and Tim Ryan.

Saturday May 21, 1994   *Duisburg, Germany*

Duisburg day one is in the books, and we had a very solid performance. The other day, we had a valuable boat meeting, in which we assessed the potential speed of this crew right now. You always race to win, but when you're facing the top talent in the world, you can't have your head in the clouds. We walked out of the room having decided that it would be considered a successful performance if we were within a half-length of Romania and overlap on Germany. After tonight's final, consider the later to be accomplished. Germany 5:27.65, USA 5:29.04; France 5:29.91. Romania did not race. This is no time to rest on our laurels. Tomorrow's Thyssen Cup is the big race, and Romania will be in the mix to liven things up some more.

I think that tonight's results bode well for the upcoming season. Last year we were over four seconds behind the Germans. Tonight it was just one and a half! However, there is no time to enjoy tonight's success. Tomorrow, we face stiffer competition. It would take a tremendous effort, but we could take the Germans. We were slightly down off the blocks, and they held a one to three seat advantage through 1000m. They held three seats or so until the 1250, where they made a big push to go out about six seats, their first comfortable lead. Heading into the sprint, I still thought we had a chance to snag victory, but Germany held on. In the meantime, France put on a terrific sprint, which we answered enough to beat them by just under a second. They, too, are certainly not a crew to be underestimated.

Looking ahead to tomorrow, I feel the key comes down to one word, ATTACK. Our race strategy is solid. We have confidence in ourselves. Now we need to go after it even harder and whip those boys. I believe that it is possible for us to cross the line first tomorrow, but it's going to take a special effort. Germany and Romania are vulnerable for an upset, but we'll have to hit every move spot on to do it.

As I lie in my bed, I try to pound the word ATTACK into my head–ATTACK the start, ATTACK the shift into race pace, ATTACK the one minute move, ATTACK the ten's, and ATTACK the sprint. I'm trying to picture the perfect race, the ideal calls at just the right time. Getting down that lane using every ounce of POWER we've got. As long as we lay down our absolute best race, we can leave the water with our heads high.

Watching the Germans in the race yesterday, I know there's a little uneasiness there. There's a small piece of them that's afraid we could go off and whip their ass like last year's heat at Worlds. Somehow we've managed to scare them, and I've got to try to use that fear this afternoon to screw with them, to take them out of their element. In turn I want to pump our eight with tons of confidence, make 'em feel like world beaters. That's what we'll need to be to pull ahead tomorrow.

The final of the 1994 Thyssen Cup in Duisburg was one of the most exciting races during my time with the national team. We traded leads with the Romanians and Germans all the way down the course. One boat would nose ahead, then another would challenge. Another boat would surge ahead, and another would challenge. For five and a half minutes, it was like three heavyweight boxers trading punches in the same ring. Our personal race was fantastic. Once we got into the fight, our determination began to shine.

Off the line, we were neck and neck with Germany and Romania. The Romanians started to grab a lead over us as we moved ahead of Germany. In the middle of the race, the Germans made their push and took over second place. But we came right back with an answer and shut them down. Moving out on Germany, we then set our sights on the Romanians. Out in front, they began to lose their momentum as the pack closed the gap. With under a minute to go, we were charging forward every stroke. Then the Romanians had a final answer to our challenge. They finished ahead of us by one and a half seconds, but we had topped the Germans by over two seconds in their own backyard. The victory over the German eight was a tremendous boost of our confidence. We had beaten them in a heat before, but never in a final. That day we learned that they were not invincible. Upon returning to San Diego for another training period, we all felt that we were in a fantastic position to light the international rowing world on fire.

Monday May 23, 1994   *Dusseldorf–San Diego*

This weekend, particularly yesterday afternoon's final, rekindled a deep, passionate desire to push myself to the absolute limits of coxing. Call it the zone, a groove or whatever. I was there, and I wish desperately to return as soon as possible. I do not want to wait another six weeks for our next race at Henley.

I ought to begin with the moments that stand out the most in my memory, the fifteen minute walk from the dorm to the course. After packing my bag for the course– tools, cox box, uniform, warm clothes, etc.–I usually save a few moments for solitary contemplation. Even if it is only a brief rest on the bed or a look in the mirror, I enjoy this last piece of true solitude. For one more moment, I am alone with my hunger.

Next, the boat meets downstairs. The power of the crew begins to work its magic. We posse up and fall into step towards the course, each individual finding his own gait. Some like to walk alone, some in groups, some with a walkman, some without. There are no consistent patterns, no stereotypes, only what you feel that day. What permeates the air is a sense of unity, a sense of togetherness. We are a military unit heading into combat.

Personally, I carried a walkman with me on each walk blasting the band "Rage Against the Machine." The music is loud, powerful, and unyielding. The music propels me forward, allied with eight giants who are about to kick some serious ass.

While we bop along, I have to restrain myself from letting loose with a war cry. I feel all the tension and the pressure of the moments ahead, the necessity of performance. These nerves must be corralled and channeled into positive energy. I feel the protectiveness of the crew, the commitment that we have for each other, a commitment for the group over the individual.

As we get closer to the course, the volume in my walkman is pushed to a deafening level. I draw deeper within myself in order to maintain focus and remain unshaken by the trivial things around me. I weave in and out of the crowd to avoid other people. I never lose sight of the guys. I stay close to use their size, their strength, and their power as more fuel for my own fire.

Soon the walk is over, and we're at the boat with only a half hour before launching. Those final minutes are spent caring for every last detail to ensure a problem-free performance. At last, we hit the water.

Unfortunately, the pressure has hardly subsided. Producing the perfect warm-up is a skill of its own, one that can often be trickier than the race. There are so many variables–motorboat wakes, other crews, races on the course, the tick of the clock, the progression of our crew, timing the final long practice start, and so on. At last, it is all done. We sit on the stake boat for two minutes before the race begins. I take another look across at the enemies on both sides.

For me, the moments on the stake boat have become the most precious. At that instant, I feel an amazing paradox of emotions. Part of me revels in the satisfaction of earning my place on that starting line. But the anger inside is ready to explode out of control and devastate our opponents.

I look down the lane ahead and review the race plan one more time with the crew. A quick glance to the right reveals our stiffest competition–Romania in lane four, mighty Germany in five. I smile at my stroke man, Chip McKibben, and revel in the moment. "Let's do it buddy," I say extending my hand.

"You know it, brother," he responds and shakes in kind. We are ready to go. At last, it is time for battle.

Looking back at yesterday's emotions, I realize that I will let nothing stand in my way of arriving at the line again and again through 1996. I hate the rigors of dieting, the ups and downs of dealing with eight egos, and any other substantial negatives related to the cox's seat. Yesterday

reminded me how all this pales in comparison to the sheer glory of racing,
the pure thrill of competition. It could be no other way. I could NEVER feel
such a rush of emotion if the job was any easier. What makes racing so glo-
rious is the strength of commitment and sacrifice that lead up to the
action. You have to endure the hard work before you can enjoy the success.

We returned to San Diego for re-selection of the eight. It was a brutal time. A massive influx of oarsmen threw the whole process into chaos. Guys from last year's eight came to San Diego for the first time, college all-stars who just finished their season arrived, and so did a few National Team members who took leave of their jobs for the upcoming international season. For Spracklen to sort through this mess was not an easy task. We trained for several weeks, and selection got ugly by the end.

During this selection process time was of the essence. In a highly shortened time-frame (less than three weeks), Spracky wanted to pick an eight and a straight four to take back to Europe. We would race and train together for a few months, and then return to the U.S. for one more extended training camp prior to the World Championships in mid-September in Indianapolis. The problem was that there were lots of guys to evaluate and not enough time to do a thorough job. From Spracky's perspective, this wasn't really a tragedy. As long as he picked the best twelve guys in the group, we could switch things around on the road. Therefore, the test for the oarsmen was to get into the top twelve. The problem that developed was that we had more good oarsmen than we did seats for Europe.

One of the newest additions to our training squad was Bob Kaehler. Like Chip McKibben, Bob was a veteran of the U.S. National Team in sculling boats. In fact, Bob and Chip were teammates in the U.S. quadruple sculls crew in Barcelona. Also like Chip, Bob was nearing thirty and in search of gold medals from World Championships. Bob added a different dimension to our crew because he was a solid blue-collar oarsman. He was always in good shape, and you could count on him to crank in the boat. Bob was an ideal member of the middle of any crew, aptly named "the engine room."

After a few weeks of testing, Spracky selected an eight and a straight four for the trip. The eight would be Chip McKibben, Fred Honebein, Don Smith, Jon Brown, Jamie Koven, Bob Kaehler, Sean Hall and Jeff Klepacki; whereas the four would include Willie Castle, Tom Murray, Jerome Ryan and Mike Porterfield. This meant that a number of solid oarsmen would be left behind, notably Mike Peterson, Will Porter, Jim Neil and Chris Swan.

The eight selected for Henley represented a strong hybrid of youth and experience. Fred, Don, JB and Jamie were repeat athletes from Spracky's crew in 1993. Like me, each of them would begin their second summer with the national team. Chip McKibben, Bob Kaehler, Jeff Klepacki, and Sean Hall were all national team veterans and Olympians. Despite these differences in experience, there was one very strong common bond–everyone hungered for their first world championship.

Once we were aboard the plane and on our way to Europe, everyone in the eight breathed a tremendous sigh of relief. The rigors of selection were over for the time being. We could focus onto the task at hand, winning internationally. On the plane ride to Europe, you could sense the enthusiasm about the summer ahead. The core of the group had been racing and training for over a year now, but this looked to be our most exciting journey. The months ahead held many surprises–Henley, Luzern, the Goodwill Games and beyond. We could hardly imagine the experiences ahead.

Monday June 27, 1994   *Marlow, England*

If rowing were a religion, Henley would be its temple. We arrived at the home of the gods around 6pm after nearly twenty-four hours of travel. The

journey was a pain in the ass, but it was very satisfying to reach our desti-
nation. Spracky arranged for us to stay with his friends, Lynne and Larry
Tracey at their estate. There is plenty of room for our whole boat here, but
the four is staying with another family in the town of Henley.

Three of the eight (Chip, Jeff and Bob) are in the main house, while the
rest of us live in a loft above the indoor swimming pool. This place is one
big playground—swimming pool, two tennis courts, croquet, bocce ball,
horses and so on. There are so many distractions, we will have to keep our
eye on the ball.

As for the racing, we have as good a chance as any other crew to win the
Grand Challenge Cup. Germany has withdrawn, which improves our sit-
uation. On Friday, Australia will race the Dutch. We race the winner on
Saturday. In the other bracket, England faces France; winner to the final.
Comparatively, we have a great shot. The British were equal speed to the
French last week in Paris, and we beat the French twice at Duisburg. The
Dutch and the Aussies are relatively unknown. When it comes down to it,
you could compare A to B to C to D and so on until the cows come in. What
really matters is how we perform on race day. Jet lag will be a factor, but
we've now got five days to rest up and get in sync. We should be ready to
fire it up by the weekend.

Last night after dinner we drove over to the course to check things out.
The boat's hopes are high. About half of us have been here before, but
everyone was equally psyched when we looked down the unique Henley
course. The racing is match-style: one on one, so the race course is only two
lanes wide, with dangerous log booms along the sides instead of buoys. One
steering mistake by a coxswain into the log booms and your crew's hopes
are all over. It was about 9pm, when we arrived at the course, so things
were very quiet. To me, it felt like a field of dreams.

Tuesday June 28, 1994   **Marlow, England**

This afternoon was our first serious practice on the famous Henley course, and it put a fair amount of pressure on me to make lots of decisions. I had forgotten how difficult it could be out there on a very narrow river with so many crews, motorboats, buoys, and log booms, plus the tricky current. In general, it is one big pain in the ass. For some reason, I also felt the additional pressure of coxing "the" U.S. eight for what seems like the first time. The only way to describe it is as if we were under a microscope. Anywhere around or on the course, I feel that all eyes are on me, just waiting for the smallest mistake, or a big one like hitting a post or crashing with another crew. There is so much going on at Henley, and plenty of "wally" crews to get in the way. This is a bit of a negative attitude, but it's my responsibility to look out for any possible problems for the crew. This will probably last for only a few days, and then I can return to fully focusing on racing. I never felt this way last season, so maybe it's just the hype of Henley. It's just another race, so let's get to it.

I feel happy with my performance thus far, but there is lots of room for improvement. Luckily, there is a week ahead to tie everything down. There are plenty of nerves jumping now, more than I'm accustomed to. That's not wholly bad. Those are the emotions that drive me to work harder and perform better. If I get too comfortable then I lose the edge. I want to be on the edge all the time. It makes me better.

We comfortably settled into our country estate living in Marlow, and the camaraderie of the eight grew by leaps and bounds. We frolicked in the pool, played croquet on the lawn, and generally had the time of our lives. The biggest danger was that we would be so busy having fun with other games that we would lose focus on the importance of the race. However, it never worked out that way. On the water, we rowed in a workmanship, determined manner. We refused to be distracted by the craziness around us. If you could do that at Henley, you were half-way to victory.

The flip-side to our happiness was the opposite direction in which the straight four was headed. The Tracey's magnificent estate was bursting by holding the ten of us from the eight, so the four took up other lodgings. They stayed in homes closer to the course, which offered far less than the incredible hospitality we enjoyed. While we had the time of our lives, they cursed us silently while stuck in their unfortunate situations. Additionally, Mike focused virtually all of his attention on the eight, so their rowing suffered. The combination of a bad living situation and virtually no coaching set them up for a poor performance in the regatta. When they lost to the British lightweight straight four in the first round, their downward slope only got steeper. This unfortunate loss also served to make relations between our eight and four that much cooler. At the time, I was so focused on the eight I hardly noticed anything outside our crew.

Thursday June 30, 1994   *Marlow, England*

I chose today to enjoy the pomp and circumstance of Henley, specifically the Steward's Enclosure and the Leander Club (courtesy of Spracky); neither disappointed. Although it was a bit hot and tiring, today was a fantastic day to enjoy the regatta. Now that it's over, I'm focused on the business at hand, winning the Grand Challenge Cup.

Henley is a spectacle not just of life, but also of British culture. The Steward's Enclosure features numerous bars and restaurants, which serve the standard strawberries and cream, etc. The dress code of Henley requires gentlemen to wear blazers and ties, while ladies must wear dresses below the knee. The upper crust flit about drinking outrageously priced concoctions and intermittently cheer, "Well rowed, well rowed." Frankly, I doubt if people are paying any attention to the rowing. Just down the road from the Steward's Enclosure is the home of the highly regarded Leander Club. The club's mascot is the pink elephant, which is plastered everywhere inside the club. Meanwhile, old rowing champions stuff themselves with more of the same British food and drink in the lush halls of the exclusive club.

All of this behavior is highly elitist, and it borders on being downright snobby. Where you are permitted entry is based solely on the badges you possess. But that is also the charm of Henley. Rather than criticize, it is better to observe and try to enjoy the festivities.

One day I have to return to Henley to drink Pimms by the bottle, eat cake at Leander, and truly enjoy all the fun of the country and the regatta.

Back here at the Tracey's, we're in store for a fun evening. Our dinner guests include Steven Redgrave and his wife. I've met him several times before, but it's quite a thrill to break bread with, arguably, the best rower of all time, three consecutive Olympic gold medals and counting.

Saturday July 2, 1994   Marlow, England

Today we faced a very stiff test in our semi-final against the Dutch. Before the race, Mike had predicted that they were the fastest opponent in our event. The Dutch looked to be a very formidable crew. Not only had we yet to fully adjust to British time, we had been struggling to deal with all the pressures of Henley. Personally, I felt plenty of mental fatigue already. Today's victory was a huge relief.

The race itself was very exciting. We were caught off guard a bit by the starting commands, and in the first five strokes we held even. In our next twenty strokes, we began to take command, and we led by nearly half a length. At the one minute mark, our set call pushed us out to a lead of six seats or a bit more. After the Barrier (a Henley marker), we extended our lead out to bow ball, almost the breaking point. The Dutch wouldn't back down. They came back to six seats, but that's as close as they'd get. In the end, the verdict was one-third of a length because the Dutch kicked into their sprint and moved on us. Mike had cautioned me against using our sprint unless absolutely necessary. Thus, we stayed in cruise control at the

end. In the process, we still managed to set course records up to two differ-
ent markers along the course.

Tomorrow we'll face the French in the Final of the Grand Challenge
Cup in the Henley Royal Regatta, one of the most prestigious prizes in the
history of rowing. If all goes as well, we should beat the daylights out of the
French. But that means nothing. We've got to earn this victory the same
way we did today–commit and attack.

Coming off the water this afternoon, we were greeted by many well-wishers
and their cheers of "USA! USA!" It was a very proud moment. Of course,
everyone now expects us to win easily, but we can't listen to that for one sec-
ond. The last thing anyone wants is a repeat of last year's Worlds–win the
heat decidedly, then lose the final. That shouldn't be the case with this crew
anyway. We are all too experienced and too fired up to do anything but win.

Tomorrow certainly provides many great opportunities. Winning that
cup etches our names in immortality alongside the greatest oarsmen of all
time. Along with victory comes its many fruits–permanent membership in
the Steward's Enclosure; offered membership in Leander Club; plus all the
*joy and celebration that go with a big win. That is **all** contingent on six*
minutes tomorrow. We need to perform. We need to attack. We need to win.

I clearly remember the van ride to the course for our final in the
Grand Challenge Cup. The trip was less than ten miles, but since the
narrow roads created heavy traffic, we had to leave several hours early.
While sitting in traffic, we blasted the radio and sang out random songs.
Since it was the day before the Fourth of July, we made sure to throw in
some patriotic songs as well. One of the guys brought a video camera
and we started making our own home videos for later amusement. I
think we even did a Chinese fire drill and ran around the car like idiots.
To say the mood was light was an understatement. Ugly American is an
accurate description.

We were all fired up to spank the French, but we had to manage the
adrenaline. If we got worked up six hours before a race, our excitement

level would peak too early. For us, singing "Yankee Doodle Dandy" and mocking the British who marched past our van eased the tension. This was our unique, fun-loving spirit. This was our secret ingredient for success. Whether or not we could maintain this attitude in the future would determine our success in other stressful situations.

Sunday July 3, 1994   *Marlow, England*

It certainly has been a GRAND day. Pun intended. We went out this afternoon and performed exactly as planned. We crushed the French–two seats in five strokes; six seats by the settle; a length by the Barrier; and open water just after that. The verdict was "easily," estimated margin twenty seconds. The French came off the water and made a claim about a stick in their rudder, but that wouldn't begin to taint our victory. We won by so much that a log in **our** *rudder wouldn't have stopped us. Spracky challenged us to send a message to the world. Today we accomplished just that.*

It is now almost midnight, and I'm ready to pass out from exhaustion. Winning is more tiring than losing. After the hoopla of the race, we spent the next few hours running around, changing into coat and tie, drinking Pimms and so on. At 6pm, it was time for the coveted awards presentation. We had a solid hour of photo time with one of the biggest cups I've ever seen and the Book of Honour, which lists the name of every crew that's won the Grand Challenge. Next we went to Leander for a few more hours of partying among the elites of international rowing. Finally, we all retired to Sentry Hill (the Tracey estate) for a great dinner of beef bourgogne and apple/blueberry crumble. After a solid week of abstention, I enjoyed some grub tonight.

Things are still a bit hazy. Our victory has not really hit me. Without a doubt, this is the biggest win in my rowing career. Now it's off to bed and I will let this all sink in overnight. One thing is for sure, my name will forever be engraved on the Grand Challenge Cup, and forever inscribed in the Book of Honour. I have proudly earned these rights and will cherish them dearly.

The Grand Challenge Cup win was our first international taste of victory as a crew. Amongst the nine of us we had won plenty of races over the years. Jamie Koven alone had won more intercollegiate races than most college programs do in a decade. But Henley was a brand-new experience. We had each dreamed of big wins, but before the Grand Challenge Cup it had been a while since the United States had crossed the line first in a major regatta. This race was the spark we needed to forge ahead. Our performance in England confirmed the crew's belief that we had the potential to be champions. We had taken the first, and arguably biggest, step towards that goal.

The 1994 Eight poses with the Grand Challenge Cup and the Book of Honour at Henley. Standing from left to right: Chip McKibben, Fred Honebein, Don Smith, Jon Brown, Annie Spracklen, Mike Spracklen, Jamie Koven, Bob Kaehler, Sean Hall and Jeff Klepacki. Kneeling Steven Segaloff.

My father and I pose in front of the famous Henley Royal Regatta course in 1994. The threatening log booms loom in the background.

We moved to Switzerland for one week of training before the next big race in Luzern. Our spirits could not have been higher. After our triumph at Henley, we looked forward to one week of training to prepare for the most important tune-up regatta of the summer, the Rotsee International in Luzern. The set-up we had in the little village of Oberageri was ideal. With the exception of a some fishing boats and a few water skiers, we had the lake to ourselves. Additionally, our hotel had a long history of housing rowing teams, so they were more than accommodating. They went so far as to cook special meals and do our laundry upon request.

The only negative at Oberageri was the ever-chilling relationship between the eight and the straight four. The seeds of the problem were sown before we left for Europe. The nature of selection is such that some oarsmen are deemed "better" than others. This automatically makes the inferior oarsmen feel like second-class citizens. The initial plan when we left for Europe was to train all twelve athletes together in one group for six weeks. We would have to split into two boats for specific races, but all training would be done together. If any members of the four began to out-perform any members of the eight, the necessary changes would be made. The psychology of the two groups was so different that this routine never came into play. Instead the eight and the four were separated entirely.

Friday July 8, 1994   *Oberageri, Switzerland*

After another typical day of training, a group of us casually sat down with Mike for an evening coffee. At one point, a waitress came to the table to tell Mike he had a phone call. A few minutes later Mike emerged and curtly announced, "It's bad news." He picked his things off the table and left abruptly. Don, Fred and I sat there not knowing what was happening. We decided it would be best to approach Mike in a half-hour's time to see if he needed any help. On our way upstairs we found that Mike had already gotten off the phone. He confided in us the details, Jeff Klepacki's father has just died.

Like a slap in the face, I was stunned. The main reason for this entry is to convey a few immediate thoughts and spill out some feelings.

What if it was one of my parents? An overseas phone call, Coach comes to knock on your door and boom, that's how you find out! It's hard to imagine a tougher scenario. It certainly makes you question the fairness of life.

At this moment, Mike just brought Jeff into his room, which is right next door to ours, to tell him the news. The thought of how close I am to that very same situation is scary. It could just as easily be me. Why not? How would I deal with it? I am as close to my parents as any other kid here, or anywhere. How anyone deals with death is unknown, but it is even eerier when you see something this close. Jeff and I are not best friends, but being in the same boat for a few months inevitably makes you tighter. I can only pray that he and his family will get through this tragedy alright.

Thursday July 10, 1994 Oberageri, Switzerland

Things usually happen in cycles and an unfortunate one continued yesterday. While visiting Zurich on our day off yesterday, JB called home to alert his father, who is a psychologist, that Jeff might be calling about the passing of his dad. In their conversation, JB learned that his grandmother, the last of his four grandparents, passed away the same day as Jeff's dad. While the death was not unexpected, it still was quite upsetting, particularly since JB does not have the ability to go back to Texas for the funeral. While the rest of the eight had pizza for dinner, I spent some time with JB talking things over. As a result of that conversation, and the general feeling amongst the boat, I have the positive overall sense of belonging or support. It's just nice to know you have the stability of eight men behind you in case of trouble.

On a positive note, a few recent conversations amongst the crew and Mike have yielded some strong prospects. In terms of boat security, it looks like there will be no changes to this eight between now and Worlds. This allows everyone to breathe easier, sit back, relax and pull. Additionally, the boat has been going well enough to give everyone high hopes for a season filled with only gold. There's still plenty of time left and lots of races to be won, but a winning attitude goes a long way.

Mike came right out and said that every man in the boat is capable of winning a gold medal in Atlanta. Personally, this means I just need to keep on doing. Every step along the path we get closer to the final eight, the one that will win the gold in Atlanta. My job is to continue to perform in the eyes of the top athletes, continue to uphold their confidence. As long as this symbiotic relationship goes forward, success will follow.

It looks like Jeff will be coming back strong. He will return to Switzerland on Thursday morning in time to compete at Luzern this weekend. Mike spent lots of time talking with him prior to departure, and he assumed that Jeff was dealing with things as best as could be expected. Mike is confident that Jeff will be ready to go for the weekend. This could put us in a win/win situation. If we win the regatta, we will be even more psyched under the circumstances. But if we lose, we would have an excuse. This is no way to look at things prior to the regatta, but it passed through my mind. Regardless, the boat has been flying this past week and if we execute properly the sky is the limit.

The passing of Jeff's father affected everyone in the boat. Rowing is such a team oriented sport that you automatically develop intimate relations with every other member of the crew. The nature of the sport turns every boat into its own family. When Jeff lost his father, each of us had to become stronger to show our support in his time of need. Our crew became stronger emotionally. We developed more powerful bonds between us. We truly rowed for one another.

Friday July 15, 1994   *Luzern, Switzerland*

We arrived in Luzern yesterday afternoon after an easy one-hour drive from Oberageri. Perhaps it's my lack of being in a city since San Diego, but Luzern appears to be a beautiful metropolis. We are staying at the Hotel Continental Park, which lies on the banks of Lake Luzern. The race course is on a separate body of water at a place called Rotsee. We ride the bus to get back and forth, which takes about fifteen to twenty minutes. The course itself is beautiful, nestled in between a few mountains that protect the water from wind.

Everyone says this is like a mini-World Championships. Realistically, it is our last big tune-up before the real thing in Indy. Since the Goodwill

Games races are only 500m and 1000m dashes it is not the same. The good news is that the eight is going along quite well. Jeff re-joined us yesterday in Oberageri, and it looks as if he has not lost a step. We did an hour's workout earlier this afternoon that went great, maybe our best row yet. Emotions are really high.

The draw was this morning and we're in good position. There are fourteen entries, which means we will race three times this weekend–heats today, semi-finals tomorrow and a grand final on Sunday. Our major competition will come from the Dutch, Germany and Romania, not necessarily in that order. We already know a little about the Dutch; the German eight contains the same guys at Duisburg, but different line-up; and the Romanian eight has a new line-up also. This is surely no time to be cocky, but we should win this regatta. If we get on the line and race to our potential that is just what'll happen. Still, it is only Friday, and there is a long weekend of racing ahead. What this regatta demands is a continual commitment and an understanding that the only race that really counts is Sunday night. We race to win every time, but Sunday is the keeper.

Saturday July 16, 1994   *Luzern, Switzerland*

Luzern has certainly been good to us as a city so far. Right now, I am writing along the shore of Lake Luzern in view of the city's famous wooden bridge. Nearby there is an ensemble band pulsing out some refreshing jazz. It is a lovely evening, and so far it has been a great regatta.

Yesterday, we raced in a heat against the Netherlands, Italy, and Germany II, three to the semi-final. The Dutch led off the line, and we raced neck and neck to the 1000m. Either they eased up or we powered through, and by 1500m we had a comfortable three-quarter length lead. Today we faced France, Romania (a new, strange line-up crew), Great Britain, Germany II and Poland, three to the final. We had a great start, one-half length by 500, and kept attacking. We did not put on any sprint *because the race was in control. This all sets up a fiery final tomorrow, USA and Germany in the middle, France and the Netherlands in lanes two and five, Romania and Russia in lanes one and six. The Germans look to be our fiercest competitors, and they are going to push us full tilt. Nevertheless, if all goes well we will be the victors.*

The point of coming to Europe, especially to Luzern, was for race experience. We are getting plenty of it. For the first time, I feel comfortable, controlled and able to truly perform at the international level. Knocking heads, and winning, against the best in the world has taught me many lessons about international racing. I cannot even begin to describe the difference from last year. For example, there is this great sense in the crew that we have accomplished nothing yet. These wins are great but there is only one that counts, tomorrow evening's final. The Germans will be tough as nails, and regardless of today's performance I do not trust Romania. We have got to go for gold. If we execute to our capability we will get it.

Monday July 18, 1994   **Aiguebelette, France**

First, the results of yesterday's final, an incredibly exciting race decided by only a few feet. Unfortunately, we had the short end of the stick and the Germans took home the gold. We led by as much as a seat through 500m, but around 600m, they started a big push, which gave them a two seat advantage. They held tough through the middle and moved out to three seats, maybe even three and a half seats around 1000m-1250m. Then we started our charge back. The lift was spirited, and we caught those bastards around 1700m. In fact, we went ahead around 1800m, but the Germans responded, took back the lead, and won by 0.57 seconds. Everyone kept their heads up because we rowed so hard for that finish, but it was a downer to lose by so little. By today, though, spirits are high, and everyone is already plotting about how we will catch the Germans.

Personally, I had mixed feelings like any other big race, especially a loss. You inevitably ask yourself what could have been done differently. Unfortunately, what's done is done. Now we have to accept these results and move on. We will race again in three weeks in St. Petersburg and get 'em then.

In hindsight the Rotsee regatta worked out perfectly to our advantage. Jeff's tragedy gave us an easy excuse for not coming through in the final. Because we could rationalize the loss, no one felt that the Germans were a better crew. The first reaction after our loss was that our crew was anxious to face the Germans at 100%. Then we would kick their ass.

This philosophy worked perfectly with Spracky's theory—you do not want to peak until the final race of each season. It was a shame to lose at Luzern, but we had a reasonable excuse that gave us hope for the future. Whether Jeff's brief absence from the crew made a difference or not, we all believed that it did. Psychologically, this allowed us to look toward the future with great hope. When races are decided by inches, the psychological edge can be worth its weight in gold. Additionally, the tragedy that befell Jeff brought the nine of us closer as a boat. We began to fight for each other, to pull for each other, and to want to win for each other.

Aiguebelette, France was our first chance to re-group since leaving San Diego. After nearly a month on the road, we could finally relax in a quiet European village and get down to training for an extended period of time. It is always fun to race, but training was what we needed at the time. The workouts would be incredibly tough, which would only improve our resilience as a crew.

Wednesday July 20, 1994　　　　　　　　　*Aiguebelette, France*

Although this seems like the toughest part of the trip, two solid weeks of intense training, it will be nice to reassess things after so much racing and moving around. Plus, the real reward will come with a gain in speed and the thrill of the Goodwill Games.

We started this mini-camp off on the right note with a very positive meeting yesterday afternoon. It began with an evaluation of Sunday's race. What happened? Why did we lose? What can we do in the interim to win next time? The result is a commitment to training at higher rates in order to race one to two strokes per minute higher. It appears that the Germans over stroked us the whole way. We need to become more efficient at 40-41 instead of 38 1/2 in the middle 1000m. Everyone seems excited to take the Germans on in the coming weeks. We want to do what's necessary to beat them. Mike also gave a brief, stirring speech about each one of us thinking about our German counterpart constantly. We each need to consider what we need to do to beat that man. If each of us beats our counterpart, we will win. It is that simple.

While in Aiguebelette our crew underwent one significant change when we switched our line-up. Jeff Klepacki, who had been rowing in the bow seat, moved up to stroke. Spracky considered doing this earlier, but Jeff's unexpected loss and his brief trip back to the U.S. made the switch impossible. Given a couple of weeks in France to get used to a different rhythm, the timing was right to give the new line-up a try. Once Jeff sat in the stroke seat I think that we all knew that we had something special. Jeff was by no means the strongest guy in the boat, but he had a real presence in the stroke seat. He could lay down a long, consistent rhythm that enabled the big guys in the middle of the crew to crank. As the line-up developed our boat's confidence grew.

Thursday July 28, 1994   *Aiguebelette, France*

Today marks the two-year anniversary of a very auspicious date. The finals of the men's eight in Atlanta, Georgia in the Olympics will occur on July 28, 1996. Around noon, six eights will line-up and race 2000m. After about five and a half minutes of battle, a new Olympic champion will be crowned and forever immortalized. It is my deepest wish that I cox that winning crew.

Aiguebelette was a relatively quiet pit-stop on our European tour. We trained hard for two weeks, put in a lot of mileage and plotted to beat the Germans. After a hectic year of traveling, it was a nice break before our next international regatta, the Goodwill Games in St. Petersburg, Russia.

Wednesday August 3, 1994   *St. Petersburg, Russia*

We have been in St. Petersburg just over twenty-four hours, and I have to admit a bit of disappointment in the host city of the Goodwill Games. Some of this is due to the fact that I built up too many preconceived ideas that were unrealistic. Still, it seems like much of the U.S. hype for the event was left in America. My hopes were high for a bit more of the royal treatment in my first international multi-sport competition. From now on it's up to the imagination.

The worst of our problems lies in the regatta itself. The course is fine, albeit a bit short since we're only racing 500m and 1000m. The real trouble is with the equipment. Apparently, the organizing committee is quite short on cash. They rented horrible boats and asked all competitors to row in similarly deficient equipment. Forget the fact that the boats are sub-standard, they do not even fit our oarsmen's bodies. At this point, it's touch and go whether the boats will survive week's worth of training and racing. Our boat leaked substantially through its sectional connection and is being repaired for tomorrow's workout.

St. Petersburg is a disappointing city. There are many beautiful buildings, and the architecture is spectacular. But the jewels of the city are buried amidst hundreds of other huge, dilapidated, poverty filled buildings. Undoubtedly, the city is experiencing incredible economic hardships since their political change. We expected a city like Prague, old and tired, but re-invigorated by rising talent, arts, and money. Instead, there are a very few wealthy individuals among the rest of the struggling population. Consequently, the Goodwill Games are hurting financially. Ideally, once St. Petersburg figures out how to create an efficient, capitalist society it will find an equally successful future.

Thursday August 4, 1994   **St. Petersburg, Russia**

Trying to stay positive is becoming harder every day. Most of us are wondering if this trip could get more useless towards our ultimate goal of winning the World Championships. The biggest consolation is that the German eight is here, too, so they are also missing key training time. What makes matters worse is that Spracky, who is usually the most positive of anyone, is lashing out at everyone.

The fun began when we all sat outside for thirty minutes waiting for a bus that did not show up. It was over an hour before we got going. When we did arrive at the course, we had to endure a few more difficulties as a result of our inadequate equipment. Don and JB are literally too big for the boat. Although we have made every possible adjustment, they will never really fit in the shell. It is simply too small.

The remainder of the problems were in my seat. I have not yet become comfortable with the steering system, and the ropes holding the rudder broke twice today. This rendered the boat almost un-steerable. When we returned to the dock for repairs, Mike responded by saying that all boats *were steered this way twenty years ago. Then he told some story about a cox whose ropes broke in the final of the Olympic eight, who adapted mid-race and won a silver medal. That's just dandy, but it doesn't help me at all.*

It just pisses me off that Mike typically bends over backwards to ensure that oarsmen are as comfortable as humanly possible. But the first time I can ever recall saying anything about my equipment, the message is, "If you can't adapt you must not be very skillful." The saving grace is that the guys are 100% behind me. Nearly everyone has said something to comfort me and let me know it is not my fault. People have warned me that Mike would press on me hard at times, pushing me to the breaking point. I fully accept that idea. You would think that it would happen during training, though, not in the final days of preparation before a race.

Saturday August 7, 1994   **St. Petersburg, Russia**

After over six weeks of training/racing throughout Europe, tomorrow is it. Today's results were mixed, but we are all fired up for the last race. In the 500m sprint event, we never got into our groove. The start caught us off guard, and we fell behind by two seats. That put us in a hole we could not dig out from. We finished third (behind Russia and Germany) and came away with a bronze medal.

Only two hours later, we got a chance at revenge in the 1000m heat versus Germany and Great Britain, with one to qualify. This time we got out well and led from start to finish. In the last twenty, the Germans called it quits and paddled in. They will be satisfied with qualifying in tomorrow's second chance race.

Now we are in a familiar situation. We beat the Germans in the heat and we feel confident that rowing our race tomorrow will give us the gold. I, for one, am not going to fall in that trap again. The Germans always raise their performance to another level in the final. Not this time. Tomorrow is our last clash before the World Championships in Indy, and I want to stick it to them. We have got to commit to excellence and finish first.

On the face of things the Goodwill Games seemed an intrusive regatta. We had to fly half-way around the world to a small course to row in horrible boats in a shortened race format that did not mean much. Little did we realize that our experiences in this regatta would lay the foundation for our success in the World Championships.

While in Aiguebelette, we spoke a bit about "the commitment," the big push we would make in a race. Every crew takes moves throughout its races. What was unique in Spracklen's approach was the way he created a move. We would employ various strategies in different races throughout the year, but in the big races each season, for example a World Championships or Olympics, we would bring out the big gun, what he called "the commitment." This move was meant to be so special, so devastating, that you could only afford to do it once or twice per year. You were supposed to approach it with such vigor that it would hurt your body to try it more frequently. The general idea was that for fifteen or twenty strokes we would all "commit" to the move. With a specific focus on one technical point, all eight oarsmen would lay down fifteen or twenty of the most powerful strokes they could possibly give.

After speaking about this idea throughout the year, particularly in France, we decided to break it out in the Goodwill Games. The important test would be in Indianapolis, but since St. Petersburg appeared to be more of an insignificant race, it would be a chance to learn something about ourselves and our competition. We would test the commitment in the 1000m final and hone it to perfection in time for the World Championships six weeks later. It worked like a charm.

Monday August 9, 1994   *Frankfurt, Germany*

Like most other end-of-regatta days, yesterday was very hectic, but also very pleasing. We raced the Goodwill Games 1000m final in a stiff headwind and utilized our focus on length and power to win by two seconds over Germany and Russia. We fell back a little in the first few strokes, but by the time we settled into race pace, we had a nose in front. Over the middle of the race, we took control and walked away. A very satisfying win, and a positive end of our racing tour.

The medal dock was pure pandemonium. First they lined us up and handed out medals, flowers and books. Next they raised the three countries' flags and played "The Star Spangled Banner," a great moment. Then things got really wild. Ted Turner and wife Jane Fonda appeared on the dock to offer congratulations, followed by Ernie Johnson from TBS Sports. We were interviewed and the cameras got a great shot of the guys tossing me in the water. In front of a national audience, the sportscasters muttered, "Hope somebody picks ol' Scrappy up!" To top it off, I was picked for drug testing and whisked off immediately after the ceremony to pee in a bottle.

This brings me to the frightening way the day started. I went out for my morning run as usual. About fifteen minutes before our bus arrived to take us to the course, I went to the bathroom and was shocked to see blood in my urine! After consulting with Mike, I took a few minutes to see the doctor, who assured me it was probably not serious. As the day wore on, my urine returned to being clearer, but I still feel a bit worried about this situation. Combining dehydration, my dieting habits, and the slamming of the boat into my kidneys I may have developed a problem. For now, there is nothing to do but wait.

My dietary problems were finally becoming evident. For months I had been abusing my body and this incident was my body's way of saying, "Enough is enough." I was frightened about the situation for a few reasons. I felt okay physically, but this was surely a sign that something was wrong internally. What compounded the issue was my fear of telling anybody what was going on. Other than Mike and the U.S. team doctor in Russia, I did not want word to get out. Mike and I had developed a father/son relationship and I trusted his judgment completely. I worried that others might take steps that would prohibit me from continuing to compete. Even my own health could not get in the way of the gold medal I sought in Indianapolis.

After St. Petersburg, Dartmouth College in Hanover, New Hampshire became our final outpost before the season's last battle. Nestled in the hills of New England, we were left to ourselves to explore new territory along the Connecticut River. Sheltered from any press, publicity or pressure, we could focus completely on working hard each day towards that gold medal in Indianapolis. After spending ten tortuous days in New Hampshire the year before, we could only imagine what a month would be like. Although Spracky piled on an incredible volume of work, the training went very smoothly.

Thursday August 18, 1994   *White River Jct., VT*

It would not be Dartmouth, nor would it be the final month of training, if weight did not become a significant issue. I feel much more comfortable this year, probably because of experience from last year and a full summer of racing. After my quick visit home and a few solid meals, I put on a few pounds before this final stretch. This morning, one month before the World Championships Final, I'm tipping the scales at 117.5 pounds. This puts me ahead of schedule compared to last summer, but still no easy task ahead. My hope is to be 115 pounds or less for the August 30th time trial, which leaves nineteen days for the final, toughest five pounds. Let it be known that no matter what, I am going to reach 110 pounds.

I can clearly remember feeling this same frustration, desire and pent-up emotion last season during this difficult time. The next few weeks will provide plenty of tough emotions, but the challenge is to stand up to adversity with courage. Already my diet has been cranked down to next to nothing–fruit, tea, a Power Bar, and maybe salad or oatmeal. I have also stepped up my running by adding a second jog three times per week. Unfortunately, the next step is not one to look forward to–Big Blue, Old Dependable, a.k.a. Ex-Lax. It is not good for my system, but it has to happen.

Friday August 26, 1994   New Haven, CT

Over the last couple of days, my emotions have really caught up with me. We raced around Europe all summer, started training camp at Dartmouth, and now we have a few days off to spend with friends and family. I feel as if my body and mind are on an emotional roller coaster. One minute I am all fired up, psyched for the culmination of racing with so many friends and family watching in Indianapolis. Next thing you know I am overcome with the enormous pressure of representing the U.S. at home in the biggest race of the year. Then I am wishing that it would all be over so I could just work, eat and sleep like normal people. There are many factors at work here: diet, stress, pressure, desire, and so on.

One of the biggest comforts is to look back at last summer's journal and see that I experienced very similar emotions. In fact, the timing is almost the same. Everything will get easier when we finally arrive in Indy because we will be that much closer to go time.

Food definitely plays a significant role in this whole fiasco. With over three weeks to go, I am hovering around or below 117. My goal was to be 115 for the time trial and it is quite attainable. The source of this stress is that there are twenty-three days to go and I have got to take off about seven pounds. It is going to happen, but it is also going to hurt a lot. This past summer has taught me a great deal about discipline and this is the final test. What worries me is that somehow I will not make it. In the past year, I have weighed 110 pounds only one day. I only have to do it one more time. I just do not want to let the guys down. They work so hard that they deserve my commitment. Already my calorie consumption is terribly low. Rarely do I eat enough for someone to call it a "meal." In that special case, I feel guilty.

What it comes down to is that this stupid dieting plays mind games. I have got to rise above it, think positive, and know that I will make weight September 18th. Forget all the fears. I have been close to 110 pounds before this summer, and that final pound or two will come off in a sweat run. It is time to lose the fear and transfer it into a commitment to victory.

Thursday September 8, 1994   Boston–Indianapolis

After almost a month in the Upper Valley region of Vermont/New Hampshire, we are finally off to our final destination of the 1994 season, the World Championships in Indy. It is hard to believe that it will all end next Sunday. Looking back on so many ups and downs, it is not too soon. This year's plane ride is quite different from last year to Prague. The journey is a very minor ordeal, as opposed to the hassles of international travel. I certainly feel much more prepared. After a whole summer of racing, there will be no surprises in the final ten days. The Germans and Romanians will be quite fast, and it will take 100% commitment on our part to win.

One very positive note is my weight. This morning after a jog I tipped the scales at 113 pounds. Ten days isn't a long time but it is plenty to finish the job. Sometimes I feel at the end of my rope, but after a whole summer of strenuous dieting, what are ten more days? Nothing. If I play this right, I can sweat to below 110 and allow myself a little room for eating the day of the race rather than going around starving.

Maybe because we have been flying all over the world as the eight I've lost the true significance of this final trip. I'm on the plane carrying the U.S. National Rowing Team to the Worlds. I am on it as the cox of the eight again. The last time a U.S. cox went two in a row in the eight was Seth Bauer in 1987-88, and that's pretty good company considering that Seth is often deemed to be the standard bearer for coxswains. Now is not a time to get too full of myself, but I do deserve a moment of pride and self-congratulations. The culmination of the whole year is right here. I made it. Now let's win this regatta and finish the season properly.

Friday September 9, 1994   Indianapolis, IN

Here is a new twist on pre-race entries, serious anxiety. After unpacking my gear in the room and a quick run, I strolled around the area to find a few necessary conveniences–coffee shop, running loop, sauna, and restaurants for celebration next Sunday. While alone in my room the anxiety attack just hit me. Out of nowhere, I felt very tense about this upcoming final. One specific memory of last year's Worlds is Spracky saying that what can be the most difficult part of big races is the waiting. Since this is my second World Championships maybe I know too much for my own good about how important our performance will be next weekend.

Monday September 12, 1994   Indianapolis, IN

Race week has finally begun and hopefully that will make time move a little faster. Perhaps the excitement of competition will drive away the diet devils that have been plaguing me this week. What I am experiencing is the typical paradox of race week. On one hand, this should be the best week of the year, the culmination of my goal to be World Champion in our own backyard. On the other hand, the stress of racing and losing weight make me want Sunday night to be here now.

The draw was yesterday and it's no big surprise. We race Germany, France, Italy, Cuba, and Ukraine; the other heat has Romania, the Netherlands, Russia, Canada, and Denmark. We are going to have to beat the Germans on Sunday, so we might as well do it twice. Plus, we have a special set of race plans for the week, including a trick up our sleeve for the final. Mike has this whole thing planned out, and it should lead us to victory. This is our regatta, our time.

Tuesday September 13, 1994   *Indianapolis, IN*

9:30am *Hard to believe that today we fight Round 1 in our battle for the World Championships. We always talked about Indy during the renegade days of the Border Patrol Boat Club when we lived at the Naval Station. Now here we are. We had a good meeting last night, the mood is loose, and we are ready to go to work on the Germans.*

Bonus. Right now, I am under weight! After my run this morning, I came in at 108.8 pounds. I enjoyed a plum, a NutriGrain bar, and a Nutrageous candy bar. I am still under weight and would rather wait to spread the eating throughout the day. We do not race until 5:18pm, so I will need the sugar later.

We leave for the course in one hour. After a short practice we will come back to the hotel for a little break, then back to the course for the race. Not many people have arrived in Indy to watch yet, but it will get more crowded as the week goes on. You can bet that Saturday and Sunday will be a madhouse. All the more reason to fire one down the course and win big.

9:30pm *We are through to Sunday's final. Just like last year, we kicked the Germans' ass down the course in our heat. Actually, they finished fourth behind France and Italy. Our margin of victory was 4.83 seconds over the field. We are not going to be fooled for a second by this result though. Those guys will be much tougher to beat on Sunday night. This time we will be ready.*

Today, we raced with our old plan of a one minute push as they figured we always do. On Sunday, we will revert to the plan we've practiced for six weeks–fifteen strokes at 250m for length and legs, then the big fifteen stroke commitment for catches at 500m. After all these months and all this racing, there is just one more time. One last shot.

In the other heat, the Dutch surprised Romania by 0.22 seconds, with Great Britain a bit back in third, Russia fourth.

Despite our successful result, I find myself in a short-tempered, bitchy, and generally angry mood. Today's results mean absolutely nothing to me. We thought Germany might play possum, but they will be screaming on Sunday night. There is no relenting of pressure, or of dieting for that matter, until Sunday.

A great down-the-lane shot of our heat at the 1994 World Championships. From top to bottom: the United States, the Ukraine, Germany, Cuba and France. (Photo courtesy of Joel Rogers)

Thursday September 15, 1994   *Indianapolis, IN*

After events of the past few days, I have reached a point of certain fear about what is happening to my body. Strangely enough, throughout this ordeal I have felt absolutely fine. Nevertheless, my body is transmitting some bad signals. There's blood in my urine again.

Getting down to weight for Tuesday's heat I felt as though my program was sensible and effective. Continuing on my runs and strict diet, I tightened the screw a bit by stopping fluid intake Monday afternoon prior to an hour run. After the jog, a chew of tobacco, and a night of dehydration I awoke at 110 pounds. A morning run took me down to 108.5 pounds so the rest of the day was spent nibbling on light weight foods and sipping fluids. At weigh-in I hit 110 pounds on the nose. After winning our heat, I made sure to drink lots of Power Ade and water. But then Wednesday morning after my daily morning jog of sixty minutes, it happened again, bloody urine. I was so upset that I nearly broke down in tears. This is the culmination of nine months of preparation and now my body shuts off. That's unacceptable.

Upon arrival at the course, I immediately sought out Dr. Jo Hannafin, who knew the background of my problem as team doctor. She suggested getting back on the liquids right up until the final for a last minute sweat run. Yesterday, I tried to drink often and by the end of the day, I felt better about the whole episode. The main point to keep in mind is that my primary focus must remain on Sunday night's final at 5:10pm. But this morning, sure enough, after my run of sixty minutes my urine contained blood again!

I'm currently aboard a 9:30am bus for the course for a day of training (two brief sessions, 8k and 12k) and a half hour run. But more importantly, I need to get the scoop from Dr. Hannafin about what's going on and what can be done. She mentioned using an IV before or maybe going to the hospital for some tests.

What's really scaring me is that while my body feels fine and mentally I'm raring to go, my insides are definitely screwed up. I am clearly abusing myself and can only hope that the damage is not irreversible. At this point, there are only three days left. Looking at racing results and from what Mike has said, this is our race to lose. From my perspective, it's important not to get too worried about this, stay focused on the race and keep my eyes on the prize. Not much longer and I hope to be called a Champion of the World.

I did not realize at the time how close I was to being declared medically ineligible by our medical staff. The doctors had discussed my case and considered a variety of options, including immediate hospitalization. To this day, I do not know why they chose not to intervene, but I am thankful they didn't. Instead of causing me any extra anxiety, the doctors tried their best to help control the situation gently.

Saturday September 17, 1994   *Indianapolis, IN*

Tomorrow marks the end of the road for this 1994 season. It has been a long year of victories and defeats, but we are ready to end with a World Championship. This season's entire experience has been great. We are all hungry for the big win. Although, I am personally a bit hungrier. My weight is right on, probably a bit under after tomorrow morning's run. That base covered, it is time to rip out one race of incredible intensity and get the job done.

Today was the first day of finals, and it produced poor results for the U.S. The lightweight eight finished a disappointing fifth, and the lightweight women's double produced the only medal of the day, a bronze. In the afternoon, the wind picked up substantially and postponed all other finals until tomorrow morning.

It was exciting to see so many fans and so much support for American boats. In the brief time I spent in the stands I saw lots of good friends. While it was nice to see everyone, it also made me a bit more uptight. Tomorrow I plan to stay away from any of that and stick with my teammates full-time. Being around other crew members helps to alleviate pressure.

There is no magic about tomorrow, although the results could make it a very special day. A win at home would be the fulfillment of a lifelong dream and the finishing touch on a good year. I hope and pray we execute and come away victorious.

After months of physical preparation, one of the keys to our race at the 1994 World Championships was our psychological preparation. The boat trained as hard as any American eight in recent history. When we arrived at the starting line on September 18, 1994 each man was physically ready to do battle with anyone else in the world. Beyond our physical preparation, though, we had a secret strategy that gave us the extra confidence to help win that race.

Throughout the previous two years of competition, we had developed a specific pattern of racing. We created a framework in our first race in 1993 and tried to consistently improve it with each test. In every race plan, we would have specific moves designed to gain ground on other countries. Amongst these various moves there would always be one extra special push towards which everyone would intently focus. For two years, that extra special push had come at the one minute mark of a race.

The moment the starter yells, "Go!" an athlete's body begins to produce lactic acid. The pain of this chemical reaction takes effect around forty-five seconds to one minute into a race. Spracklen's theory was that all oarsmen feel the same pain and receive a message from the brain that says the body needs a rest. Mike thought that if we could push through this chemical pain at a time when every crew was hurting, we could benefit. Thus for two years our American eight would make a move at the one minute mark. Our ploy got to be so well-known that other countries' coaches even told Spracklen they knew what we were doing. In Indianapolis, we used the suspicions of others to our advantage.

In our heat on Tuesday we rowed a typical race plan, including a push at the one minute mark. According to the German racing-style in previous years' heats, we figured that if we could get out early the

Germans would back off and save their fighting for the final. There was little to gain by showing all their cards early in the week, and they would not want to give anything away. By 500m into the heat, we had total control and the Germans backed down. Little did they know that the trap had been sprung. The Germans, the Romanians, and any other country watching assumed that we would be following our usual race plan in this regatta. That was just what we wanted them to think.

For the past two months, we had been practicing a new set of moves, one quick burst around the 250m mark, approximately forty seconds into the race and then our big push at the 500m mark, approximately one minute and twenty seconds. If executed correctly, this would be the equivalent of throwing a brutal one-two punch combination. It may seem like the smallest of differences on paper or even in reality on the water. But where it mattered most, in our heads, the difference was enormous. When we went to the line Sunday evening, it was like having the trump card up our sleeve. We believed that this tactical adjustment could catapult us into rowing history.

The start of the 1994 World Championship eights race was truly bizarre. That year the international rowing body had changed the official starting commands. Instead of a rhythmic set of commands, "Attention. Set. Go!" this year they would say, "Attention. Set. (Variable Pause) Go!" That variable pause could be an instant or as much as five seconds. The change was instituted so that no one could anticipate the starting command and everyone would have to wait until the word, "Go!" to start. The men's eight is the last race of the regatta. By the time of our final, the starting procedure had already produced mixed results. In the women's single, the odds-on favorite, Silken Laumann from Canada, was disqualified for two false starts. In each instance, she anticipated the variable pause too early and jumped out of the blocks. In the eights race, we encountered similar results.

In the men's eight final, the Ukrainian crew arrived at the line with one false start for a prior rules violation. Each crew is allowed one false start, so Ukraine was now one step away from disqualification. We sat one lane away from them completely focused on our own race plan. At the start, we had trained to squeeze after hearing the word "Set." Basically, we were betting that the variable pause would be minimal. We were wrong. The starter left a huge pause in between "Set" and "Go!" during which we, and a number of other crews, jumped the gun. Four out of six crews received false starts, including the Ukraine. The officials told Ukraine to leave the course and now there were only five boats left to battle for the championship of the world.

The mass false start took away some of our focus for an instant. While paddling back to the line one of the guys said, "Oh man that sucks. Ukraine doesn't even get to row."

Just as quickly another oarsman answered, "Fuck those guys man. This is our race to win." The fuse was lit again. The false start turned out to be a blessing because it loosened up everyone's nerves a bit. We would have to be more patient for this set of commands, but this would definitely be the real thing.

When the starter announced, "Attention. Set. Go!" we got off the line cleanly. We did not take the lead immediately, but within twenty seconds we were close to first. At 250m, we threw the first of our two punches. Our bow leapt out a few seats and you could feel the confidence flowing. Already, we had the opposition on the ropes and we were just getting started. There were only a few strokes in between the two moves, so when 500m came along, everyone was really gunning. We had a lead in the World Championship, and we were not going to look back.

The second punch was more lethal than the first. Our strategy was working as planned. By the end of the second move, we had nearly three-quarters of a length on the field, a huge margin. As we moved through the half-way mark, the lead had grown to open water, truly unbelievable. No matter how much confidence anyone had prior to the race, no one could have possibly thought we could lead the race by that much.

Throughout the second 1000m it became clear that we had paid a large price to get that lead. The critical question was–could we hang on?

The closest three crews, Netherlands, Romania, and Germany all charged together. Then the Dutch pulled away from the pack. They moved only inches at first, but once they felt themselves gaining on the lead, those inches turned into feet. In the final 500m, the finish line could not come soon enough. The Dutch put on an incredible charge, which fell short by 0.6 seconds. We held on. I still maintain that we could have held a lead for several hundred meters more. The adrenaline rush from leading a race of that magnitude is tremendous. Each oarsman can see the opposition move, and they know just how much they have to give to hold onto a lead. The Dutch made a great run at us, but they would have had to find another gear to pass our boat. They could not do it.

We crossed the line six-tenths ahead of the Dutch and became the Champions of the World for 1994. In the process, we had set a new world record of 5.24.50 The dream was reality.

Monday September 19, 1994   *Indy–New Haven*

We pulled it off. Yesterday, we were crowned 1994 Champions of the World, the fastest boat on the water, and in fact, the fastest boat ever recorded over 2000m! It has been an incredible, indescribable twenty-four hours filled with emotions I cannot even begin to comprehend. After big races you always feel a tremendous rush of emotion. Over this past season, we have enjoyed the thrill of Henley and the Goodwill Games, plus the disappointment of Luzern. But nothing can relate to winning a World Championship. We achieved the ultimate. There is one more step, an Olympic Gold, but only time will tell.

Afterwards was absolute pandemonium. The crowd was going nuts while guys pumped their fists in the air. All the time, their muscles screamed that we had to move. Eventually, we paddled back to the 1500 meter mark for the victory parade, and then onto the dock. Once on shore, the scene got even weirder and wilder– fans cheering, the medal ceremony, bands playing, and lots of reporters firing questions. Even now, I am quite numb to the idea that we won. I felt so elated after fulfilling a life-long dream, but at the same time disoriented, as if to wonder, what's going on here? It was also very interesting to notice all the different reactions people outside the boat displayed. At least five cried on my shoulder thanking me for the win. I only got choked up once, when Jeff cried during "The Star Spangled Banner" thinking about his father.

Last night was fun but it, too, had this surreal quality to it. The whole world seemed to be in a haze. Too much of my time was spent as host and I ate too much, which made me nauseous. I just cannot shake this weird feeling, the finality of the whole situation, the closure of a dream. It has been a while since I have had much alone time, particularly without any pressure. There are so many competing emotions that need to settle in I would like to take a moment to sort it all out.

For the rest of my life I am a World Champion. No one can do anything to ever take that away from me.

As a humorous footnote, we all did not enjoy the same festivities while celebrating our championship that night. It was a Sunday night, and the city of Indianapolis was ill-prepared to handle throngs of international athletes spilling out into the streets. After months of intense training everyone is ready to blow off steam. Alcohol is consumed in abundance. The police were called in after midnight to control the crowd and settle down everyone's enthusiasm. At one point, a canister of tear gas was opened that quickly did the trick. Some people did not react very well to that police action. One of those people was Sean Hall.

Somehow Sean got mixed up with a few policemen, words were exchanged and Sean spent his first night as a world champion in the city jail. The director of USRowing got the phone call and bailed him out in the early morning.

*Driving toward the finish line at the
1994 World Championships. The Dutch bow in lane 4 is charging ahead in the
final strokes of the race. (Photo courtesy of Joel Rogers)*

*Raising our hands in victory on the medal dock in Indianapolis.
From left to right: Sean Hall, Fred Honebein, Chip McKibben,
Bob Kaehler, Don Smith, Jon Brown, Jamie Koven, Jeff Klepacki
and Steven Segaloff. (Photo courtesy of Joel Rogers)*

Celebrating in the waters of Indianapolis after our World Championship.
From left to right: Sean Hall, Chip McKibben and Steven Segaloff.
(Photo courtesy of Joel Rogers)

When the Head of the Charles Regatta came around in October, you could sense that something was different. I told myself that I was not any different than the guy I had always been. Winning a world championship was not going to make me different over night. I convinced myself that this was not the time for jubilation because a bigger task still lay ahead, Olympic victory. But no matter how many times you tell yourself these things, an ego is hard to control.

Through my experiences with success in the sport of rowing, I have a better understanding of the athlete's role in American society today. Rowing is a low profile sport with few perks, almost no money, and relatively no fame factor. At best, other rowers at regattas might recognize American Olympic champions. Yet winning and the glory it brings with it still encourage an individual to develop a pretty substantial ego. By winning in Indianapolis, we got a small taste of what it is like to be a highly regarded athlete. I can only imagine what real superstars enjoy on a daily basis. It doesn't surprise me to see that most professional athletes consider themselves above society's rules.

The Head of the Charles is the most popular rowing event in the United States. On the third weekend in October thousands of people descend upon Boston for this yearly ritual. Although most of the quarter million people in attendance use the weekend as an excuse to get together with old friends and party hard, some people actually pay attention to the rowing.

After two days of heavy drinking, the city empties out onto the banks of the Charles for another day of partying and a few hours of race watching. The highlight of the racing is not the actual competition, but the crashes. Head racing format is unique in that each boat races against the clock. Approximately fifteen seconds separates each crew in an event, and the goal is to cover the course as quickly as possible. Inevitably, faster crews will pass slower ones, and when you throw in bridges and curvy rivers as variables, crashes are part of the game.

At the Head of the Charles, the Championship Eights are the featured event, and therefore saved for the last race of the day around 4pm. By this time of day, a lot of the fans that have stayed around long enough to see the racing are drunk, passed out, or not paying attention. As we sat in the river basin preparing for the starter to call us to the line, I could still think of more than a few people on the bank who would be paying close attention.

Our world championship crew came to race in Boston that weekend in a very odd position. In head races, the crews are seeded according to past performance. Each boat crosses the line in single file and race etiquette calls for the crew being overtaken to yield way. Because we had not competed in the 1993 Head of the Charles, our crew was relegated toward the back of the pack. We had to start in the twenty-seventh position behind every crew that had qualified in the previous regatta. We had our work cut our for us.

Despite our precarious position, we could have won that race on the fumes of excitement that lingered from Indianapolis. We weaved in and out of crews with ease and had a fun row. We won the race with room to spare. The positive spirit we had worked to build all year was now flourishing.

Another popular American fall regatta is the Head of the Schuylkill in Philadelphia. The Schuylkill does not have the same tradition as the Head of the Charles, but the regatta is always fun in its own way. The style of each regatta typifies the attitude of each city. The Charles in Boston highlights an elitism founded in the ivy towers of Harvard University. On the other hand, the Schuylkill in Philadelphia is a tough, gritty regatta where you make sure to drink a six-pack within an hour of getting off the water. When a group of us decided to throw a four with coxswain together for the race we didn't anticipate any trouble. We were wrong. Entries for the regatta had closed a few weeks earlier, and race officials vehemently refused entrance to any late-comers. Despite the officials denial of our plea, we snuck into the race anyway.

The four that had gathered included Jon Brown, Jeff Klepacki, Sean Hall, and Don Smith. All of us lived near Philadelphia, and we thought it would be fun to jump in a boat and race. Without an entry, we had to use some connections. An old college teammate of JB's, Paul Urfel, had taken over as head coach at Franklin and Marshall College nearby Philadelphia, and he was at the regatta with his squad. They had entered two coxed fours, but were about to cancel the second entry. JB told Paul our dilemma, and Paul turned over the entry to us. The coxed four would not be a very competitive event, so we looked forward to a fun race.

Franklin and Marshall is not a rowing powerhouse, so we started towards the back of the pack. We paddled down to the starting line and found our position in line, directly behind the University of Pennsylvania. Penn is consistently the fastest college crew on the

Schuylkill River, so when they saw "Franklin and Marshall B" pull up behind them they could care less. Little did they know who was representing Franklin and Marshall B that day. In rowing, the faces of elite athletes are not so popular that you would recognize national team members or even Olympic Champions. While we sat there waiting, Penn did not have a clue.

The guys in my boat wanted to have some fun. We did not want to cross the start line and run right into Penn, so Jeff told me to say something to the Penn coxswain. Feeling every bit the cocky World Champion I politely said, "Excuse me, Penn. When the race starts could you please move to starboard when we pass you?"

The Penn crew was so startled, they shook their heads and didn't say a word. The only look I caught was a shrug of disbelief. "Tell 'em again, Scrappy." Jeff said. "I don't think they heard you."

"Yo, Penn. When the race starts, can you move to starboard when we pass you? Thanks." Another shrug.

Minutes later we crossed the starting line. We cruised through Penn so fast I don't think they had time to say "Franklin and Marshall." We passed over half the field and won by well over a minute. There's not much more fun than that.

Soon after the race had ended, though, word got back that there was some sort of problem. The rumor was that we were disqualified and the officials would like to see us. Dispirited, we sought out the chief referee. What ensued was only too symbolic of how rowing's glorious tradition can also hang around its neck like a ball and chain.

The chief official first made it clear that we were disqualified. The funniest part was that the timekeepers had triple-checked the results because they could not believe that Franklin and Marshall B had won the event by such a huge margin. Then, officials heard that the Franklin and Marshall crew was a bunch of national team guys. The official thought our behavior was immature and embarrassing. They told us the night before that we could not race. So why did we break the rules?

We argued with race officials for over half an hour, but they wanted nothing to do with us. We didn't care about being recognized as winners, nor could we care about taking home the big silver platters given to Head of the Schuylkill champions. What was flawed was the attitude conveyed by officials at this regatta or numerous other rowing events where tradition hurts more than it helps.

In what other sport would race officials blatantly deny entrance to its top athletes? Can you imagine the NBA asking Michael Jordan to sit out a season because he didn't get his entry form in on time? Or the PGA asking Tiger Woods to sit out a golf tournament? It simply makes no sense to me how an American regatta would not enthusiastically greet its top rowers. The ultimate irony in this particular situation is that the entry deadline occurred on nearly the exact day that the five of us won a world championship while representing our own country.

One of the most unfortunate byproducts of our championship season was the effect it had on my friendship with Tom Murray. When I look back, it is instructive for me to see how winning can go to your head. I have learned that you gain insight about yourself in both winning and losing in athletics.

My friendship with Tom Murray went back to 1987 from the Junior National Rowing Team selection camp. Our friendship blossomed in college. Throughout my four years at Cornell, Tom and I were the best of friends. We rowed together, pledged the same fraternity, and shared many experiences. Tom spent an extra semester receiving his degree, so there was only one semester when he and I didn't hang out all the time. For the summer after my college graduation, Tom, a close mutual friend of ours, and I drove around the United States for six weeks. That fall, he moved back to Philadelphia to resume training while I went to Washington, D.C. for my job.

Ever since the selection of the 1994 eight, my friendship with Tom was on the rocks. Our boats traveled together for part of the season, but the four was miserable and racing poorly while the eight was winning and loving life. This did not make for good company. Our separate crews grew further apart, however, I clearly remember a special moment just after the race.

When we returned to the boat storage area in Indianapolis, there were tons of people there–friends, family, media, and so on. We walked our shell through the crowd and returned it to its place, shaking plenty of hands along the way. After the boat was stored, more people crowded in to greet us and congratulate us on the big win. In the midst of all this confusion I saw Tom. Surely he was still depressed about his crew's disappointing ninth place finish, but he still managed to put on a smile. He held up his hand for a high-five, but I was far more fired up than that. I jumped up into his arms and he gave me a big hug for a second. After putting me down, I said, "None of this would ever have been possible for me if it weren't for you. Thanks." He nodded in approval and prodded me to go out and enjoy the celebration. That was the last spark of our friendship for a while.

After the season ended I had time to reflect on the events of the preceding year. Two dominant themes emerged. First, I wondered how much longer my body would tolerate my dieting. Second, I tried to analyze the elements that led to our success in order to reproduce victory in the years to come.

Saturday November 5, 1994   *New Haven, CT*

I will readily admit that I have developed a full-scale problem. Psychologically, this has become a monster that haunts me virtually every waking day. Physically, though, the situation isn't any better. My visit to the doctor the other day did not turn out too badly. It showed that my body is simply unhappy with the way it has been treated and I have developed anemia. My mind can deal with the intensity but my kidneys may not. Talking this over with some people they readily suggest changes in my lifestyle—no more soda, caffeine, chewing tobacco, laxatives or dehydration. What they are saying makes sense, but it is not that easy to change overnight. I have become rather set in my ways and change does not come easily. Worst of all is my attitude about the whole thing. I do not really care about after-effects, as long as I survive through July 28, 1996. Writing that out may sound stupid, but those are my true feelings. It is nearly impossible to provide an explanation, but my vision is so blurred that I cannot see much beyond that day. A part of me feels that if I reach such heights I will be able to conquer any other obstacle.

Monday December 5, 1994   *New Haven, CT*

"Success is a journey not a destination." This thought-provoking saying caught my attention in September in Indianapolis. I passed a billboard bearing this statement several times each day as our bus drove to and from the site of competition. Throughout the week's racing, I scoffed at the author, thinking to myself that he had it all wrong. There are certain achievements in life so momentous that their accomplishment renders you an immediate success. In that precious moment, you have arrived at success. My personal victory that week forced me to re-evaluate the quotation's validity.

. On the final day of racing, our crew won the World Championships, a feat accomplished only three times in twenty years for the United States. A brief five and one half minute race catapulted us into the history books forever. We secured our spot alongside the greatest American crews of all time. We had arrived at success. Or had we?

How do five and one half minutes change the type of person you are? How does such a microscopic amount of time affect the way people will view you for the rest of your life? The answer is that it does not. By no means is success achieved in that brief span of time. Success is earned by commitment to a goal day after day.

This saying's anonymous author was correct in his/her evaluation. One may become a success by means of one moment in time, but almost always that moment took exponential hours of hard work and careful planning to achieve. It follows that true admiration should be strictly reserved for the brave souls who find the guts to live up to a standard of success day after day.

Chapter 3: 1995

In 1995 we returned to San Diego just after the New Year. Mike had given us a few months to ourselves, but it was time to renew our commitment to winning. The Pan Am Games were scheduled for March, and we would need a few months to get back into racing shape. As defending World Champions, we would have to be prepared to face many challenges ahead. We were kings of the hill, and everyone in the world would want to knock us off.

The plan was to train for a few months, select boats for the Pan Am Games in March, return to San Diego for another month of training and re-selection, then head to Europe for a few months of intense racing leading up to the 1995 World Championships in Finland in August. 1995 would be an important year for many reasons. For starters, we were the defending champions. Now that we had reached the top, we could not be content to train as hard as in the past. We would have to find another gear. Secondly, this was the season before the Olympics. How we finished 1995 would set us up for the most important year of the all, 1996. 1995 would also provide plenty of racing experience, so that in the Olympic year we could hide out in San Diego and train our guts out.

One huge bonus for the 1995 season was our boathouse situation in San Diego. Since we left in June of 1994, the Olympic Training Center had finished the boathouse. We finally had a place to call our own. There was no plumbing for the first month, but the storage space was preferable to the old shipping containers we used to inhabit. As the year wore on, the Olympic Training Center blossomed. By April, the dorms and dining hall were ready. The oasis in the desert was real after all.

Very early in the year Mike called a meeting for the World Championship eight. After a typical day of training, we gathered in the Olympic Training Center boathouse for a discussion. Mike started out by talking about our positive attitude through the daily grind, and our cohesiveness as a group. Next came an analysis of the year ahead. "We make all decisions as a group, so while I am organizing this year's program I would like your input. We have had many invitations to race around the world and I would like to know where you would want to go. We can go to Germany, Portugal, and other places. It is important that we gain race experience this year so I want to know where you want to go. How do you want to do it?"

I remember feeling very proud of myself at that moment. As a member of the crew, I had equal say in how the year would progress. The greatest coach in the world was asking for our opinions. Where would we race? What would we do? It really made you feel important.

Next, Mike moved onto the meat of the discussion. Very bluntly he began, "The eight is a very tough event. It takes a special crew to be able to win race after race. You should realize that you are going to lose again some day. Right now, you feel as if you are on top of the world. You feel unbeatable. Maybe you won't lose. Maybe you will go on to win every race, and boy would that be great. But the odds are that you are going to lose some day. I am not saying that to make you feel bad, but rather to prepare you for that moment. Because if you do lose, then what matters is how you deal with it. If you let that loss nag at you, it will spiral downward very quickly. That is bad news. Just remember that there is only one race that really matters, the Olympic final in Atlanta. We want to win every race we are in, but the one in Atlanta is the one that matters. Remember that."

As I sat there listening to Mike speak of our impending obstacles I heard him but I really was not listening. "Whatever," I thought. "We are the fastest crew in the world, and we don't ever have to lose again. We were the best last year, and we will be the best this year." It's too bad my ego blocked out Mike's voice of reality because he could not have been more right. Throughout the season Mike's words of warning would continue to ring in my ears.

Monday January 30, 1995   *Chula Vista, CA*

*It's a long road ahead. It seems like just yesterday we cranked it in Indy, and now the intensity has returned already. These days we're going through the final stages of selection, i.e. coxswains. There is really nothing to fear because my seat seems secure. Nonetheless, any time my seat is at stake, I feel the same anxieties as anybody else. On a run the other day, I figured out that another cox has sat in "The Eight" for maybe five **practices** since Spracky has been here. I was supposed to be in the eight tonight, but by helping the pair with coxswain I was late so Pete Cipollone took my spot. It was absolutely nothing when compared to the big picture. But I'm so used to sitting in that seat, so uptight, and so competitive, that it drives me crazy. Controlling that energy, though, and directing it positively I can be even better.*

Pan Am selection was a complicated matter because Spracky wanted to send a small squad of athletes. His idea was that most of us would compete in more than one event. The top guys stayed the same. The eight would row unchanged from Indianapolis. Fred and Don would double up in the pair without coxswain event. Chip, Bob, JB and Sean would row double up in the four without coxswain. Jeff would join Tom Murray, Chris Swan, Jim Neil, and myself in the four with coxswain. Jamie Koven did not double up because he was still studying at Brown. He would take his spring break to join us in Argentina, hop in the eight, and return to school.

Wednesday March 9, 1995   *Orlando, FL*

The past twenty-four hours have certainly been a memorable experience, busy but memorable. Soon after arrival, we started out on a hectic pace that has slowed briefly for now until our 9:30pm departure for Miami. From Miami, we'll have a ten-hour flight to Buenos Aires to think all we want.

This morning, the day began in earnest by 9am. Our first appointment was the processing room. It was great fun and hopefully just a taste of a fantastic event next year in Atlanta. They give you a shopping cart and fill it to the brim with gear—shoes, socks, shorts, pants, shirts, sweats, etc. Guys say it will be this and much more in the Olympics—rings, leather jackets, etc. Just talking about Atlanta gives me goose bumps.

Now I am sitting in a quiet spot in the hotel lobby forty-five minutes before departure time. A moment for a few reflections. One lesson to be learned here is how easily you can be distracted in such situations. All these extraneous activities take your focus away from the action at hand. Granted this is a far more pressure-free environment, but it is still notable. Second, the Olympic hype is big and it is only going to get bigger as Atlanta approaches. The subject is constantly being brought up. The stakes are huge. The more I hear the more I want to be a part of it.

At the Pan Am Games, like the Goodwill Games the year before, my enthusiasm greatly exceeded the reality of the conditions. In Argentina, our housing accommodations were slightly better than military barracks. Two bunk beds crowded a cold, cement room that would comfortably house one person. If all four residents put their bags on the floor, there was nowhere to step. The four of us also shared a tiny bathroom, where the shower was a rusty spigot that sprayed all over the walls.

The rowing course, and its related logistics, were no better. We endured a one-hour ride each way to a lake, which was often un-rowable due to high winds. In our little time there, we were usually restricted to one small area of the lake.

To make matters worse, during the week before competition, I caught a nasty case of the flu. I spent a few days sleeping off a high temperature and growing incredibly bored sitting in an uncomfortable room all alone. Fortunately, I recovered in enough time to get back into the boat and take care of business.

Monday March 20, 1995   *Mar del Plata, Argentina*

It is all over. We are packed up and on our way home today. We just checked out of our rooms, and now there are a few final hours to enjoy the Argentinean sun and beach. Luckily, yesterday's two gold medals are weighing heavily in my bag, so my mind can rest easily. Plus, a great steak dinner last night still has my belly full.

It was 5am when yesterday's alarm went off and the sky was dark. We lumbered out of bed and into the bus. After the much too long one-hour bus ride, we arrived at the course for a full morning of racing. Surprisingly, the flags were hardly blowing, the water was nearly flat, and we had the week's best water.

The coxed four race was at 9am, the third event of the morning. The guys were all fired up. The eight, we hoped, would be an easier win, so this was one to go for. We were out in lane five, while Canada over in two was our main focus. My role was additionally limited because coxswains in a four-man boat lie in the bow facing forward. This awkward position prevents a cox from seeing beyond his periphery unless he makes a big head turn which typically disrupts the balance of the boat.

In the race, we had a rather powerful start and were lead dog by 500m. Canada was right there with us, but we entered the middle 1000m with confidence. It felt like we found a pretty solid rhythm, and we began to pull away from the pack. Everything was going well. As we entered the last

500m, Canada was out of my picture without turning all way around, so I had more or less written them off. We had decided amongst the crew that if a boat started to move back into us Jimbo would shout out their name to give me a warning. We entered the last 250m, and I still thought we were in pretty good shape. With less than twenty strokes to go I peeked over to lane two, and here come the Canadians charging like a mad bull. We crossed the line ahead of them by one-half second. What a bummer. We won a gold medal, but it wasn't very satisfying.

The eight raced around 11:40am. In the meantime, Don and Fred won the pair by six seconds. Our group saw this race as redemption for our other mediocre performance. Unfortunately, this was not to be either. Jeff, Don and Fred felt groggy from their earlier races; JB, Jamie, Bob and Sean felt residue from yesterday's straight four; and Chip had not fully recovered from his case of Argentinean flu. This left the eight clearly a step or two away from peak performance. We still had a great start (six seats within twenty-five strokes) and easily moved on to open water by 500m. From there we didn't really stick, the lead moved to one-third to one-half open water, but the piece lacked the special feel of a big race win. Throughout the regatta, our boats came down to the level of the competition. That may be a bit of a harsh critique of a highly successful team performance, but you have got to aim high.

Our performance in the Pan Am Games was symbolic of the danger of the year to come. In my two events, we raced down to the level of our competition. Canada fielded an average squad and we managed to beat them modestly. At top speed, we should have been lengths ahead, but instead ended up only seconds ahead.

One of the hardest things in sport is the ability to go out and win consistently. Getting to the top of the league is one thing, but staying on top is another. When you have never achieved a number one ranking there is a burning desire in your gut to get to the top. In every race, you work your ass off to get to the top. You will sacrifice anything to be the best. If you don't succeed, you go back to training and work harder. You try anything to find that little bit which will make you the best. Then suddenly, you break through and earn that gold medal. You are the best in the world. At that instant, you are forever changed as an athlete. That one big win always sticks in your mind and you think, "Nobody can beat me. I am the best." When those thoughts go through your mind, you are in trouble. The trick is to regain the hunger you had as an underdog.

Thursday March 30, 1995   **Chula Vista, CA**

I have had a super past couple of days by keying on one simple thought–STAY POSITIVE. Early on in my return to rowing, the main thing I kept repeating to myself was to remain positive in the boat. During this past week, rather than mope about getting back to training, dieting, and pressure I returned to positive thinking. I lead a great life–few financial concerns, lots of friends, healthy body, good family, cox of the fastest eight in the world, and so on. The list continues long enough to outweigh any negatives. Relax, enjoy your lifestyle and have fun; everything else will fall into place. Keeping this simple rationale in my head has allowed me to forget petty negatives and have fun again.

Monday April 3, 1995   **Chula Vista, CA**

We raced in the San Diego Crew Classic this weekend. The regatta committee organized an exhibition race between us and the Canadian eight. What was so remarkable about the regatta was the way in which people fawned over our eight. We rarely get to compete in American regattas, so there is usually little interaction between us and the American rowing community. For two days, people were very excited to see the fastest eight in the world, an American eight at that. Little kids walked around, pointed at us, took pictures, and watched our every move. It is amazing that I remember going to races and doing the same thing as a kid. I simply cannot get over the fact that people now look up to me. Young coxes looking up to me! The overwhelming emotion I feel is GRATEFULNESS.

The race itself also proved to be a good experience. We were up against a Canadian crew that was clearly outclassed, so Mike came up with a smart race plan. Instead of racing at our usual thirty-eight strokes per minute and higher to struggle to win by as much as possible, Mike challenged us to take our usual start, get clear water as soon as possible, and then drop the stroke rating as low as possible and still move away. Mike wanted to see how powerful we could make every stroke

What happened was a very positive experience for the whole boat. We took off out of the gate as expected and had open water by the one-minute mark. The rate came down to 34 strokes per minute (spm) by the 500m, 33 spm by the 1000m and 31 spm for the last 500m. The whole time we continued to move away. We only won by seven seconds, but at such a low rate, it really allowed the guys to execute our rhythm—power and rest. Each stroke was an exercise in cranking. It was also quite a sight to see so many people along the shoreline marveling at our speed.

When we left the water, it was a time to enjoy the popularity of being the U.S. eight. It was the one of the few times in any year that you feel so proud to be a part of the eight.

The past few days were fantastic and provided a perfect segue to the next six weeks of tough training before our first important racing trip to Europe. When we line it up in Essen in May, we need to send an immediate message to the boys around the world that we have only gotten faster. We are only going to get faster in the next eighteen months. No more losing. Ever.

There is a definite reason for the sudden swing of overwhelming positive attitude in my notes after our return from the Pan Am Games in Argentina. After the Pan Am competition, the body that oversees international rowing (FISA) made a decision with tremendous ramifications on my life. Based on the advice of a committee of doctors from around the world, FISA officially changed the minimum weight for male coxswains from 50 kg (110 lbs.) to 55 kg (121 lbs.). I have no idea whether my personal physical problems were ever a part of these discussions, but the timing seems more than coincidental. Regardless, my life had changed drastically.

Suddenly, the relentless pressures of dropping so much weight disappeared. The demons of weight loss and the medical dangers I had faced in the past vanished. I could live a semi-normal life again. The new weight was not automatic for me. I would still have some work to do to lose weight, but the difference was significant.

Soon after FISA's announcement of the coxswain weight change, it was time for initial selection of the 1995 eight. Logistics for the 1995 season were tricky since the eight would spend almost two months apart from the squad, after which there would be an opportunity for re-selection before the World Championships. Additionally, because Jamie Koven was still in school, we would use Mike Fillipone as a fill-in for Jamie for our first trip to Europe.

Early in the process, it looked like our magical line-up from Indy would not survive. Jeff and Sean had been struggling in training, and Mike Peterson had resurfaced as a favorite for the eight with his new pair partner Adam Holland. It's worth noting that this partnership was founded on necessity, not friendship like the Peterson-Will Porter pair from 1993. Will Porter retired prior to the 1994 World Championships. Adam was an intense competitor and a very powerful oarsman. Nevertheless, he was one of the most eccentric personalities I have ever met, and not surprisingly, a Harvard graduate. For example, after a particularly upsetting defeat later that summer Adam carved a Chinese symbol into his forearm to commemorate the occasion. Personality quirks aside, when it came time to choose the eight, Adam and Mike were a full length faster than Jeff and Sean. By choosing Adam and Mike instead of Jeff and Sean, Spracky was making an affirmative decision to value Adam and Mike's raw power more than the rhythm benefits of Jeff and Sean.

Wednesday May 3, 1995   *Chula Vista, CA*

This afternoon Spracky officially announced that Mike and Adam would replace Jeff and Sean in the eight. For some reason, though, after the announcement Spracky sent the eight on the water in an old line-up that included three guys who wouldn't join us in Europe–Sean Hall, Jeff Klepacki and Jim Neil.

As we carried the boat down to the dock, the mood was so heavy you could feel it draping over your shoulders. It was as if three men were doomed, and yet they had to endure one more practice in a boat in which they would not compete. A very sad scene. To make it even worse Jeff sat in stroke and was staring at me the whole time. Throughout the workout, he would make comments like, "I can't believe I'm not going to stroke this boat," or "I don't know if you're in the position to say anything, but if you could talk to Mike, I'd really appreciate it."

During the warm up, I strained to see into Jeff's eyes. He wore a pare of blue-tinted Oakley sunglasses that shielded his eyes a bit, but not completely. The boat pulsed on, and the power surged while everyone's muscles cranked together. I saw streams of water flow from each of Jeff's eyes. Either he was sweating directly from his eyes, or they were tears, more likely the latter. On this note, we're off to Europe to defend our crown.

The 1995 season was designed to provide us with a lot of international racing experience. Our plans called for more than three months on the road–three weeks of training and racing in Europe (Germany, Portugal, then back to Germany); two weeks of training in Georgia leading up to the U.S. National Championships; then back to Europe for more than two months of training and racing culminating in the World Championships in Tampere, Finland.

Friday May 19, 1995   ***Essen, Germany***

Tomorrow is our first day of racing here in Essen. Sunday afternoon is the one that counts, but we want to be at our best in both races tomorrow. No reason we cannot send a clear message from the start that we are faster than last year.

Yesterday before the afternoon workout Spracky gave the boat a slight tongue lashing about FOCUS. He offered that the boat had become distracted, and we needed to funnel our concentration in order to stay on top. We deserved the lecture, and the results were immediate. Guys were much more fired up and the boat started to take off. Yesterday was the first time we measured pieces in time, and the results were mixed. We really don't have an idea of this boat's capabilities. The only way to truly know our potential is to line it up on Saturday and Sunday and see what happens.

After a quick afternoon talk from Mike, we had our first serious boat meeting last night to talk over the state of affairs. Mike began by speaking about the word "focus," and then asked each oarsmen for his own definition. After going through each member of the crew, Mike asked me and I answered that to me focus was different. It is my job to pool together everyone's thoughts and provide a boat focus throughout practice and racing. Mike then responded that my answer was correct. He added that there is only one person who can talk about the boat focus and bring it all together, and that was the coxswain. Mike's further comments expanded on this idea of the role of the coxswain and how important it was for me to make clear, accurate calls. At first I felt as though he was putting additional pressure on my shoulders to pool the boat together. Right after the meeting, I felt pretty nervous. In one sense, Mike had put most of the pressure on me. Already, though, I am growing more confident that Mike has faith in my job. Just do my best.

In our first race I got a glimpse of Adam Holland's racing style. His behavior in his first race as stroke of our eight should have sent me a signal about the craziness ahead. Our morning heat contained the German eight, the Romanian eight, and a few other boats of lesser significance. With three boats to qualify, this race was really a formality before the afternoon final.

The start was unexciting, and once we settled into pace, we were only a few seats off the Germans with Romania trailing by half a length. Throughout the first half of the race, we battled back and forth with the mighty German eight. We would make a move and draw back to even, then the Germans would respond and move back out a couple of seats. All the while, the Romanians did just enough to hang out in third and not waste any excess energy. Around half-way, the Germans made a surge. You could hear their coxswain calling a push and they moved out to over half a length. Once they knew they could take seats on our crew, they called the rating down and eased off the pressure. They had the measure of our speed and were quite content to paddle the last few minutes of the race. Somehow Adam was in another world.

When the Germans backed off, we began to move through them with ease. What seemed to escape Adam's mind was that our surge forward had more to do with their reduction in speed than our gain. As we passed the Germans, Adam leaned over and shouted, "See you later assholes!" Not only was this an incredibly bush-league thing to say, it only served to infuriate the Germans. They took the comment in stride and tucked it away for use later that day.

As he yelled, I remember thinking to myself, "What the hell is he doing?!" Chip, sitting in the seven seat directly behind Adam, nearly lost control of his oar because of shock. For such an intelligent young man, Adam showed his total lack of common sense in big-time international racing.

Saturday May 20, 1995   Essen, Germany

After our first big race of the season, the dream of an unbeaten eight is over. Today, in the first day of the Essen Regatta, we finished one length behind the Germans, and a few seats behind the Romanians. It sucked because we had the lead through the 1000m mark. We led by about three to four seats and seemed in command of the race when the Germans threw in a huge push. They started moving and never stopped. The Romanians, who had fallen far behind, came back from over a length down to sprint through us in the last twenty strokes.

There are lots of reasons for our loss, but mostly a drop in rate and a loss of confidence. When we did not answer their move, we stopped attacking and the Germans were filled with fire. You could come up with plenty of other excuses–new line-up, jet lag, and so on. They all amount to nothing. When it comes down to it, we dropped the ball.

Luckily, tomorrow is another day and we get another chance. Tomorrow is the money day and victory brings with it almost $1000 per guy. Last year, we had an average race on Saturday night but came through for the big one on Sunday with a narrow loss to Romania and a big win over Germany. We can beat those bastards, but we'll need to have a great race.

It has been a bit of a bummer to drop this first one after all our past success. I knew it would be awfully hard to stay on top, but I did not figure on giving a length away in our first title defense. The important thing is to stay positive and respond tomorrow. We are fortunate enough to have another chance so we need to make the most of it. Our boat meeting was still positive, and we have come up with a more specific, more attack-oriented plan for the Langnese Cup. Let's hope for the best.

Monday May 22, 1995   *Oporto, Portugal*

We had a much better final yesterday afternoon in Essen, but it still wasn't enough to take home the $8,000 prize, which has now eluded us for three straight years. Just like last year's final, it was a gutsy race but again we came up short and finished third. We had a decent start and a relatively powerful middle of the race, but we're just not able to throw a knock-out punch in the home stretch. One thing we have on our side is time. Let's put our nose to the grindstone and get down to it. We have got to keep taking steps forward if we want to enjoy the success of last summer.

The next week in Portugal was meaningless. We expected to race the German eight, but instead found a junior crew next to us on the line. It was fun to visit another country, and we needed another week to put things together. Essentially, Portugal was a break before another important race in Ratzeburg. Given a week of training, and based on Adam's antics in Essen, Spracky put Chip McKibben in the stroke seat. In hindsight, it's easy to say that the crew had already begun to miss the steady rhythm of Jeff Klepacki from the 1994 season.

Suddenly, our race in Ratzeburg took on tremendous importance. The first two weeks of our racing tour had been a failure. Now we had to respond by showing some boat speed. Unfortunately, it seemed that the rowing gods were not with us in Ratzeburg. What seemed like an unpleasant trip developed into a downright mess.

For starters, it rained nearly every day we were there, which forced us to suffer through damp clothes on and off the water. Additionally, we faced a series of frustrating equipment problems. On our first day on the water, we were caught in a storm that nearly sank our boat. That flooding broke my cox-box, which prevented me from communicating with the crew because the sound system was washed out. And to top it all off, I ran over a submerged log that broke the fin off our boat, thus requiring additional repairs. As race weekend approached we were longing for the bright, sunny days of San Diego.

Saturday June 3, 1995   *Ratzeburg, Germany*

Today was the big day. After three weeks of training/racing around Europe, today's 2000m test against the German eight was supposed to be a key piece of the 1995 season. A win would send us back to the States more fired up than before about winning throughout the rest of the season. The boat had been getting better every day, and we were all primed for a good race. As the boat sat on the start line, you could sense the positive energy and the desire to reach our potential. Then disaster struck.

This year there are new starting commands. In a normal FISA starting situation the starter polls all the crews, "USA. Poland. Russia..." Next, he says, "Attention." raises a red flag, at which point our bow man yells, "Up!" to alert the crew that we're going, then the starter yells, "Go!" and simultaneously drops the red flag to signify the start of the race. In practice, Mike often tests our concentration at the start to try and trick us to go off differently. The goal of the exercise is to squeeze the first stroke at any sound made by the starter after "Attention." Unfortunately, we have never trained to go without any sound because that's what happened this afternoon.

When we pulled into the starting blocks, things started to get weird when the officials rearranged the lane order. We were supposed to be in lane two, Poland in three, Russia in four, Germany in five, some other crews on the outside. When I pulled into lane two, the officials yelled, "United States, lane one. United States lane one." I obliged and then saw that the order had been changed–U.S. in one, Poland in two, Russia in three, Germany in four. Once we were locked in the gate I asked the guys to sit forward and get ready in case anything strange happened.

The aligner was sitting in lane zero and he began to give orders to even up the boats. The guys were sitting up at the ready position, but blades were not fully buried. At that instant, I remember thinking that this could be a home job and we should be ready. Adam muttered something inaudible from the bow, and a second later the Germans blasted away. Our first two strokes were virtually useless, and five seconds into the race we were a length down. We got our act together as quickly as possible and went like hell in the first 500m. Still, we were stuck in too deep a hole and couldn't recover. Despite a valiant effort by the guys we lost by 3.5 seconds. Immediately, I shot my hand up in the air to signify a protest. Then things started getting really crazy.

Before the race, the officials asked us and the German eight to pull into the victory dock regardless of the outcome for a ceremony to symbolize the unity of the world through rowing. When we pulled into the dock, unity was certainly not at hand. I asked the guys to keep quiet for a minute and let me do the talking. After weeding through a few officials who did not speak English, I stood in the middle of a pile of blazers and began arguing. Before you knew it, there were a few TV cameras, plenty of photographers, and a growing crowd scene. I pleaded my case with the officials and it became readily apparent that they were not going to do anything. I could file an official written protest, but it was not going to change a damned thing. Ten minutes after our landing, they handed the cup to the German eight. Spracky eventually came onto the dock and advised me to not pursue the protest.

We then had to endure an hour long ceremony, which included the planting of a tree and a bunch of German speeches. At this point, the German race organizers started kissing some serious ass to make up for the error. They invited us into a posh club and stuffed us full of free Langnese ice cream (especially Magnum bars) and fancy cakes. Tempers were still on the rise, but what could we do? Two hours after landing on the dock, we got back in our shell and made the ten minute paddle back to our boathouse at the Ratzeburg training center. Mike was waiting on the dock. He looked quite unhappy and then bad got worse.

We all felt bad enough about things, but Mike managed to make each of us feel much worse. I cannot remember being so down after any race in the past three years. He started out by claiming that we should have just sat on the stake boat rather than pull away in such circumstances. Later in the meeting, he criticized me for not listening to the start of the previous races, among other things. As JB later said to me, "You took the brunt of most of his venom." All I can say is that now I am pretty bummed out. I should have taken control of the boat at the start and prevented the crew from rowing. Rather than get too uptight, I have got to put it aside and concentrate on doing better. George Patton once said, "Success is measured by how hard you bounce back when you hit bottom." Let's just hope that this race was the bottom, and we will bounce back.

As we got on the plane to return to the U.S. for a few weeks of training, the mood was less than positive. In fact, spirits were as low as they had been in my time with the team. For the first time in my experiences with these guys we weren't having fun. Of course, it's no coincidence that we weren't winning.

The word that kept popping into my mind was chemistry. An often used term in sports journalism, chemistry describes the intangible relationships amongst teammates. More often than not winning teams have good chemistry, while losing teams don't. Rowing, no less than any other team sport, thrives on chemistry. In my mind it was chemistry that vaulted us to victory in Indy. Flying home from Ratzeburg I know that I wasn't the only one who wondered if our current crew lacked this special ingredient.

Returning to America was a step on the road to recovery. After a few weeks of bad weather, bad food and none of the familiarities of home, it was a relief to get back to the United States. Additionally, we welcomed back Jamie Koven, who joined us in Georgia and was put into the stroke seat of the eight to try to give the crew some spark. Nevertheless, our crew continued to battle bad attitudes. Losing had made us all surly. We recognized the problem, and even tried to work it out ourselves through boat meetings. In the end, though, winning would always provide the best cure.

The following week I was officially named to the 1995 U.S. National Team, my third in a row, and it felt like any other day. Essentially, the pressures of performing at a consistently high level took away all the excitement. A quick trip to nearby Gainesville, Georgia, site of the 1995 U.S. National Championships and the 1996 Olympics, would change that.

Monday June 19, 1995   *Gainesville, GA*

Our crew arrived yesterday afternoon at the Olympic site. We have talked about Atlanta and this spot since the first meeting I attended in New Brunswick more than two years ago. It's quite a feeling.

This afternoon we made our way down to the course. It turns out that not only is this event serving as a test for American rowing, but also for the whole Olympic Games. This is the first pre-Olympic event for any sport in the area. As a result, the organizers and volunteers are going crazy. This regatta boasts the highest volunteer-to-athlete ratio I have ever seen, not to mention security.

The course, and the whole site for that matter, are absolutely gorgeous. The cost of all facilities is reported to be about $15 million, and it is not hard to see how much effort has gone into the construction. The course is perfect, and the newly built boathouses are enormous. There are plenty of tents for medical facilities, sponsors, and anybody else with a stake in the regatta. Judging from this afternoon's scene, this week will be fun and next summer will be the event of my career. God willing I will be a part of it.

Stepping back from the big picture for a minute, tonight is a good time to describe the crew. After a few ups and downs of our latest journeys, the group is starting to gel. The reasons for this rebirth could be many–Jamie

Koven's arrival, home soil, attention from the American rowing community, or something else. Right now, we are hanging out after the evening row. The sun is on its way down so the air is very temperate. The boys just cooked up who knows how many pounds of pasta and are stuffing themselves with plenty of food. We don't have our TV hooked up, so our time is spent talking, reading, writing or just hanging out. It is a very friendly environment, and we all still enjoy each other's company. Plus, there are no other adults around, so we're free to behave as childishly as expected. The favorite evening activity is using the home owner's motor boat, strapping me to an inner tube, and seeing what it takes to knock me off of that thing at break-neck speeds. It could be a long nine weeks in Europe. This is our last chance to recharge the batteries before the trek. Things are coming together slowly but surely.

At the 1995 U.S. Nationals, our rising spirits turned into improving boat speed. Or maybe it was the other way around. For the first time in a while, we performed up to our potential. The competition wasn't that stiff–some other American all-star crews, Canada and the Ukraine–but we throttled everyone. We leapt out to a three-quarter length lead within one minute and finished more than six seconds ahead of the field. In addition to being a feel-good win, the race sent us off to Europe with newly found confidence.

The first stop on our next European tour was Henley, so we returned to the friendly confines of the Tracey estate. The Grand Challenge Cup presented an interesting test because there were only two entries, us and the British. Although it might have been nice to race more than once, our battle against Great Britain would definitely test our mettle. Without a doubt, the entire Henley crowd would be shouting for their home-town boys to wallop the Yanks.

The first stroke of the 1995 Grand Challenge Cup. From left to right: Adam Holland, Mike Peterson, Bob Kaehler, Chip McKibben, Jon Brown, Don Smith, Fred Honebein, Jamie Koven, and Steven Segaloff.

Monday July 3, 1995   *London–Zurich*

We pulled out a win yesterday in an average performance. Any win is going to boost the spirit of the crew, but yesterday's race also gives me a "Whew, did we escape that one." sort of feeling. Henley's unique one-on-one style of racing means that anything can happen, so we ought to be thankful that it did not happen to us.

The crowd was primed for our race. Thousands of British fans had turned out to see their boys dethrone the current world champions. Henley is a unique spectacle for fans due to their proximity to the boats. On the land side of the log booms, fans stand within ten feet of the racing. On the far side of the race course, hundreds of fans tie their motorboats to the posts that separate fans and racing crews. From an athletes' perspective, you feel as if the crowd is right on top of you. Today that whole crowd was cheering against us.

The first half of the race went just as planned. We took a small lead at the start, a bit more by the one minute push, tied the record to the Barrier, and set the record to Fawley where we led by one length. At that point of the race, we could either break the Brits and cruise away or let them stay in the race. They started a charge and kept on moving throughout the second half, but never got within a half-length. The crowd was going nuts on both sides, the sound so deafening that my calls went unheard. At the finish, we became only the second crew to break six minutes by finishing in 5:59, one second off the course record. It seems like emotions were mixed by the victory. Guys were pumped by the prestige, but it was not too convincing to allow for sheer joy.

We had very little time to celebrate our second Grand Challenge Cup victory. Luzern was only one week away, and that regatta would be our final tune-up prior to the World Championships. Our performance at Luzern would indicate whether or not we had truly improved since our last bit of European racing.

Our racing in Luzern started off fine. In our heat, we faced an easy draw and moved ahead without trouble. Our semi-final race was a different story altogether. Because of a higher than usual number of participants in the men's eight event, we had to race a semi-final comprised of six boats, where the top three qualified for the next day's final. In our pre-race talk, Spracky warned us not to take the field lightly and assume that we would qualify. In the race itself, we stumbled through the last 500m and dropped from a solid second place position into fourth. We had failed to qualify for the final and the crew was devastated.

Saturday July 8, 1995   **Luzern, Switzerland**

If this season has a low-point, or if my rowing career on the National Team, has a low-point, today may be it. First, a catalog of a few of my current emotions–shame, humiliation, despair, wonder, sorrow, and more shame. After three years with Spracky, this is what it has all come to, a B Final. He always says that when things go wrong you should blame yourself first. As I sit alone in this dreary, cramped room that is exactly what is going through my mind.

Looking back at my performance, there is nothing glaring that sticks out as horribly bad. My calls were on, and I tried to keep the boat informed of where we were and what we had to do to qualify. However, the fact that we were rowed through is evidence enough that I screwed up in some way–motivation, clarity, emphasis on the power/length of the sprint, whatever. We did not qualify, and by that fact alone I have got a lot of improving to do.

Where do we go now mentally? Mike has been warning us for a long time about lack of focus and how little it takes to drop the ball. Today we learned how painful that can be.

Somehow, someway we have got to pull our heads out of the gutter and respond. Seven weeks from tomorrow are the World Championship Finals. If we can rebound and come back with a gold there it will all be all right. If the ball continues to roll downhill, though, next year is going to suck. Already Atlanta looks like a million miles away.

In closing, I find some solace in a Thomas Paine quotation–"I love the man who can smile in trouble, that can gather strength from distress, and grow brave from reflection. 'Tis the business of little minds to shrink; but he whose heart is firm and whose conscience approves his conduct will pursue his principles unto death."

Sunday July 9, 1995   *Luzern, Switzerland*

*It is 11:45am on Sunday morning, and I have already finished racing for the regatta. Never in a million years did I, or anyone in the boat for that matter, consider **not** being in the final. Perhaps that is all part of the problem.*

Going down for the 9:15am B Final, I still felt all the shock and humiliation of a champion defeated. We usually joke in the boat that no one goes to get a hot dog during the men's eight final. For our final today no one got a hot dog because (1) the hot dog stand was closed that early; and (2) most people were still asleep in bed.

[8pm Same Night] As this day of unpleasantness turns into night, I find myself trying to avoid a valley of depression. We had a squad meeting to discuss race results to date, our outlook for the future, and logistics for tomorrow. Spracky was frank and honest so his words hurt. The gist of it was that the eight has performed slightly better than mediocre all year, dating back to the Pan Am Games. The good news is that he believes the top crews this year are well within our range. If we re-commit and re-focus for the next five weeks in Oberageri, we can retain our crown as World Champions. Make no mistake about it, this will take very hard work.

When we arrived in the small village of Oberageri after the debacle in Luzern, we arrived at a true crossroads. The schedule called for five weeks of training in Switzerland before our departure to Finland and the 1995 World Championships. We could either sulk in tears of self-pity or try to resurrect some feelings of championship spirit. Despite the obstacles we faced as a small group of bored, homesick Americans, we somehow found a way to find a winning spirit.

Perhaps the key to our revival in 1995 was the fact that we finally found ourselves in an environment without distractions. In fact, Oberageri was so quiet and so dull that we only had each other to keep company. For four and a half months before Oberageri we had very little time to catch our breath–Argentina, California, Germany, Portugal, Germany, Georgia, England, Switzerland. We had been on the road racing for months and had forgotten how to settle into a solid training regimen. Oberageri provided the perfect remedy to the preceding peripatetic months. All we had to do was think about getting fast again.

Sunday July 23, 1995   *Oberageri, Switzerland*

   On a lighter note, there's a very funny contest afoot during our six weeks of solitude here in rural Switzerland. We are so bored that we created a facial hair growth contest. The results are hilarious two weeks into the process. Most of the guys took the opportunity to grow all sorts of crazy stuff. Even Spracky joined in the fun with a style that looked like something from a Gilbert & Sullivan opera. I tried to do whatever my slow-growing facial hair would accommodate. The end result was playfully dubbed the "Jelvis" look by the guys, as in "Jewish Elvis." I guess the name fits because I have pointy sideburns that end somewhere near my chin.

The growth contest at Oberageri in 1995. From left to right: Jamie Koven, Mike Peterson, Steven Segaloff and Jon Brown.

An added benefit of the solitude of Oberageri was something none of us had ever experienced under Spracky–multi-boat solidarity. Based on our poor performance at Luzern, Spracky trained all twelve oarsmen together and held off selecting the eight as long as possible. Consequently, there was no hierarchy of boats and less tension amongst athletes. And more importantly, both the eight and the four gained valuable speed.

Of course selection is never easy. Even though both boats would head to the Worlds in good shape, the eight would have a far better chance to win and it would always be the glamour event. As selection drew to a close, things became interesting. The port side was chosen rather easily; it would be a repeat of the 1994 eight–Jon Brown, Fred Honebein, Bob Kaehler, and Jeff Klepacki. Starboard, on the other hand, was another story. Don Smith and Jamie Koven were assured of their spots, and Sean Hall moved into the third spot. That left Chip McKibben, Tom Murray and Mike Peterson to battle for the last seat. There was very little difference between all three guys, but in the end Mike Peterson earned the seat. Thus the U.S. eight was off to Tampere, Finland with only one change from our 1994 World Championship crew, Mike Peterson in for Chip McKibben.

All things considered, the eight felt solid. We hadn't dwelt on the disappointments from earlier in the season, but at the same time, we all remembered the sting of Luzern enough that we didn't want to fail again.

The 1995 World Championships were more intense than those I had experienced in 1993 or 1994. It had been a long racing season, and we had endured a lot of ups and even more downs. After weeks of isolation in Switzerland we wanted to battle it out. Meanwhile, our competitors were under more pressure than usual because this World Championships served as the primary qualifying regatta for the 1996 Olympics. Because the Olympic Games restricts the number of entries in all sports, almost all of the crews that would compete in Atlanta would be determined in Finland. Countries had an alternative means of qualifying for the Olympics, but those routes were more risky. For example, the top eight men's eights in Finland would automatically qualify for Atlanta. The final two spots would be determined in the summer of 1996 at a special regatta. The Olympic qualifying pressures didn't affect us because the U.S., as host country of the 1996 games, was guaranteed an entry in each event.

Because Olympic qualification was up for grabs more countries than usual entered the men's eight event. Accordingly, in 1995 we would have to progress through three races to retain our world title–a heat, a semi-final and a final. In the days leading up to our first race, the crew continued to gel. When we drew the Germans for our heat–the third time in three World Championships–everyone grew more excited.

Monday August 21, 1995　　　　　　　　　　　　*Tampere, Finland*

I think our crew is poised for a good week of racing. We have to be careful to cover every base and make no mistakes–false starts, crabs, whatever. In these rough conditions, anything can happen. We need to be prepared to deal with whatever fate throws at us. That being said, I think the guys are primed for a strong performance. Their legs are fresh and ready after all those weeks of getting their asses kicked in Switzerland. We have worked hard on a race plan, and it has come together quite well. No real surprises. We have tightened up all of our previous weak spots, and I feel as if the whole course is covered. The semi-final will be more attacking, and the final will contain the big commitment we'll need to come out on top.

Mike has told us throughout the past week and a half that he would not have done anything differently with this crew during the season. We had to have a natural progression in speed or else our confidence would have suffered. As we enter the big week, the crew is peaking at just the right time.

He is the psychological master. If he has played this one correctly, and I sure hope he has, we should return to the middle of the medal dock on Sunday. One thought that keeps going through my head is that no American eight has won back to back world championships. If we do cross the finish line first on Sunday, we'll have the opportunity not only to be the best in the world, but perhaps one of the finest American crews of all time.

In our heat, we took a solid first step in defense of our title. We got out of the gate fast, took a big lead on the Germans and responded to every move they made with a power surge of our own. The result was a comfortable victory and a trip to the semi-final round of racing.

Our draw for the semi-final in the 1995 World Championships was ideal. We faced Australia, Canada, Great Britain, Poland and Romania, with three to qualify for the final. First, we avoided the two crews we considered to be most dangerous–Germany and the Netherlands. Second, we had a golden opportunity to exact revenge on Australia and Romania, two crews who had knocked us out of the final at Luzern. In one race, we had a chance to improve our racing confidence and exorcise a recent demon.

Thursday August 24, 1995   Tampere, Finland

The semi-final is behind us, and there was no repeat of Luzern. In fact, the results couldn't have been more opposite.

In the late afternoon a vicious rainstorm wreaked havoc on the course and postponed racing for over an hour. We spent our spare time jammed into a shipping container with lots of other American teammates. Despite all the distractions, we kept our focus and took to the water with determination. The heavy rains subsided, but a wet mist still enveloped the warm-up zone. As we sat on starting the line, there was a slight chill in the air, but the water was nearly dead calm.

Off the line everybody shot out like a cannon. Romania might have led us by a nose early on with Canada and Great Britain just behind us. Poland and Australia fell back, and I never heard from them again. At the one minute mark, Canada made a move. What would you expect from Spracky's old crew? We pushed ahead. We started our surge at the one minute mark, and kept cranking. We never looked back and were never again challenged for the lead. We cruised across the line over two seconds ahead of Romania, while Great Britain followed for the third and final qualifying slot.

In the other heat, Netherlands, Germany and Russia battled nose to nose for 2000m. I have not seen the times but heard that the Dutch nipped the Germans by about 0.6 seconds with Russia not too far behind.

Now we have two days to paddle around, calm down the nerves, and go for the one that counts on 12:30 Sunday afternoon. After tonight's racing, I can proudly say that we are on track to repeating. The guys feel like they had a strong race without burning the big commitment around 750m and without committing to the sprint. Come Sunday, we will need every trick in the book to take the title.

Got a nice package from a friend from home yesterday. He wrote a long letter that included a quotation is from Hakeem Olajuwon of the two-time World Champion Houston Rockets. When asked about his team's perform-ance, the Dream responded, "NEVER QUESTION THE HEART OF A CHAMPION." That's just the way I feel about our boat. We took our licks throughout the season–Essen, Ratzeburg, Luzern, and so on–and now that championship time is at hand we are on form. It is going to take our best race to win on Sunday, but if we do perform to potential, we will be the first men's eight in American history to win back to back world championships.

After all the ups and downs of a long season, we had one last chance to make the year a success. If we could win the World Championship Final, the rest of the season would be ancient history and we would be remembered as the first American eight to win back to back World Championships.

Our race plan for the final was slightly different than years past. Throughout our training in Oberageri we had implemented a strategy that called for several aggressive moves throughout the 2000m course, especially in the middle and later stages of the race. This was a significant change in strategy from Indy in 1994 where we focused heavily on the early stages of the race. Our strategy in Finland seemed solid, but our execution on race-day was not perfect enough to get the job done.

Monday August 28, 1995   *Helsinki–Dublin*

The season is over and my third World Championship is history. Sad to say that we didn't accomplish our goal of repeating as World Champions. We finished third in a wild, windy, and rather disappointing race.

Off the line, we fell slightly behind Russia and even with Germany. During the big commitment, we started to row down Russia and Germany. We barely nudged in front. A small crab, or "shipwreck" as Spracky calls them, slowed us down considerably, and we lost some momentum. Still in the hunt at 1000m, we passed Russia and maintained contact with Germany. We attempted to execute our big commitment call to climb back into the lead, but encountered another "shipwreck." At this point, Germany moved decisively ahead and the Netherlands came through us into second. Entering the last 500m, we would need an incredible sprint to win, but passing Netherlands was not out of the question. Unfortunately, the boat could not sustain enough momentum to move out of third. When the dust cleared, Germany won in about 5:53, Netherlands two seconds back, USA two seconds behind them. Russia was two seconds behind us. A very slow time, which substantiates the rough conditions.

I am now aboard a KLM flight en route to Dublin for a week's vacation with Don, Jamie and Tom. As always, after a season ending regatta I'm struck by a wide range of emotions–disappointment, sorrow, anxiety, frustration, relief, and so on. In the long run, I hope that the events of this past season will make us hungrier for the big year, 1996. I hate to think you've got to lose before you win, but who cares now. 1995 is history. We are on to 1996 and the final golden dream.

Our performance in Finland was the perfect example of the delicate balance between confidence and over-confidence. We arrived at the regatta an angry crew. After a dreadful performance in Luzern, we were anxious to prove to the rest of the world just how good we were. We went to Finland as defending world champions, and none of us were ready to give that title back. Another country would have to take it away from us.

In the opening races, we came out with guns blazing. In both the heat and the semi-final we looked as formidable as ever. It looked like the '94 World Champions were not dead just yet. Word started circulating that we were faster than the '94 crew. People said that this was the best American boat in recent memory. That is just what killed us.

No member of our crew would tell you he felt over-confident in the 1995 World Championship final. Each one of us was fired up to defend our title, and we believed we should win. The difference was in the word "should." In 1994, we believed we "could" win, not should. That difference is not a small matter. We tried just as hard in 1995, we attacked and we gave 100% effort. But there was some small psychological breakdown that prevented us from retaining the title. As soon as we started listening to people saying how good we were, or how we were faster than 1994, we were cooked. Without that red-hot desire to prove ourselves, we missed the extra zing that would earn a gold medal. We settled for bronze.

The off-season between 1995 and 1996 was anything but restful. A combination of our mediocre performance in the 1995 World Championships final and the upcoming pressures of the Olympic year made everyone that much more uptight. After Finland, we had two months off to lick our wounds from racing. The goal of this period was to relax and have fun for a while. Ideally, we would return to San Diego refreshed and re-focused on the task ahead. Unfortunately, the sloppy events of September and October provided anything but relaxation.

Fall racing looked to be innocent enough. As the U.S. eight, we had two commitments during those two months. First, the Head of the Ohio in Pittsburgh held a charity race against Canada to benefit the burn unit of a local hospital. A few weeks later, we were scheduled to defend our title in the Championship Eights race at the Head of the Charles. Both of these "fun" races turned into big headaches.

The Head of the Ohio is one of the few regattas where national team rowers are treated like superstars. The regatta puts on a great show and takes fantastic care of the international talent. From the moment we were picked up at the airport, we enjoyed parties, museum tours, riverboat rides, and so on. The hospitality alone is worth the journey. In 1995, we took full advantage of the regatta committee's generosity. We ended up spending more time in bars than in the boat. All that drinking did little to help our racing.

On Sunday morning, we competed in the Canadian-American challenge, a 1000m race. Throughout the weekend, the rowing took a back seat to the fun we were having, and the race itself was no different. We paddled out to the middle of the river with the Canadians and waited for race instructions. An official pulled up in his motor boat, told us to get ready, and suddenly yelled, "Set, Go!" We were definitely caught with our pants down, and in such a short race there was no chance for recovery. The Canadians whooped us good and my immediate reaction was,

"Spracky is going to be furious. He will never understand that this was an unimportant race." Moreover, in my heart I knew that I would bear the full responsibility for the loss, and rightfully so. It is my job to get the crew ready to start. I should have recognized our disadvantaged situation and yelled for the crew to stop immediately. It was Ratzeburg all over again. Forget the fact that this race may have appeared irrelevant–it would matter to Spracky, and that is all that really matters. The disaster at the Head of the Ohio was just the first log on the fire that began to burn in Spracky's furnace. We were about to pour gas on the flames.

The 1995 Head of the Charles was far different than the year before. In 1994, we rode the waves of success from Indianapolis into Boston. Our boat had so much positive energy that the boat nearly floated atop the water. In 1995, we faced a variety of difficulties.

Our troubles leading up to the Head of the Charles started weeks before the regatta. In Finland we had decided, as a boat, that we would all participate in the race. The only person who would not be involved was Spracky. This was not simply an agreement to race, but a commitment to training for a week before the regatta. The announced date for our return to San Diego for 1996 was November 1st, a few days after the Charles. This timing could not have been worse. Since full-time training would begin immediately after the Head of the Charles, few people wanted to give up their last week of freedom by meeting in a self-run training camp to prepare for a "fun" regatta.

The other problem was that the stakes of the 1995 Head of the Charles had been raised significantly. Two notable international crews had decided to make the trip to Boston to challenge for our title. Moreover, they were coming to America early to train properly for the race. The full Dutch eight, second in Finland, made plans to come to Dartmouth for ten days prior to the Charles. Additionally, an all-star line-up of Germans and Canadians joined forces to form a composite crew. What was supposed to be a joy ride against the top American college crews had now become a major international event.

Still, the threat of international competition did little to motivate our group. As the coxswain, I was stuck with the thankless task of organizing our crew's training plan. What I ran into was a logistical nightmare. We had to find a training site, a boat, oars, accommodations, food, and various other details. As I made a few rounds of phone calls, I ran into several roadblocks. Forget the rowing logistics, the crew could not get together in one location. Some guys were amenable to anything, but about half the crew had some type of training requirement. One guy was taking the GMAT the day before the race five hours south of Boston; two other guys already made plane arrangements to be in Boston two days before the race; and yet another could not leave Philadelphia until two days before racing. I tried to work out a variety of compromises, but with little success.

I was greatly frustrated by the situation. Then I was surprised at home by a phone call from Spracklen asking how things were going. I told him of my dilemma, to which he calmly asked, "Right then, please give me everyone's phone number." What followed was a round of phone calls, during which most guys were chewed out thoroughly.

In his various conversations, Mike made some of the strongest accusations I had heard in his tenure. Among the snippets, "You are acting like a bunch of losers...You don't want to win anymore..." The result of his venom was an outright threat—win the Head of the Charles or lose your monthly funding for October. Now this "fun" race had become a financial ultimatum.

After a few more days of phone calls, we arranged for a mini-camp in Princeton, New Jersey. We would have to use substitutes for a couple of days, but it was better than nothing. When we finally gathered in New Jersey, it was no happy reunion. Instead, we arrived as an angry group who had to band together and row fast or else. In my opinion, this was part of Spracky's master plan anyway. If he had to get us to hate him in order to respond then so be it. As long as we won in Boston, he could care less.

We had finished exactly one practice in Princeton when I was hit with another obstacle–a death in the family. My grandmother had been sick with cancer for years. That afternoon, as I had rowed up and down Carnegie Lake, she passed away in her rest home. I felt awful about her death, but at the same time thankful that I was able to be with my family during the mourning period. In the past, I had feared that this inevitable phone call would come to me in some faraway country where I could not leave. At this moment, I could get in my car and drive three hours back to my home in Connecticut in time for the funeral. Out of fear of Spracky's recent wrath, I called him immediately to let him know why I had broken training. "Family matters are the most important, Steven," he consoled. "You should go home." Two days of mourning went by, I hustled back up to Boston and jumped into the boat.

Flash ahead to the warm-up zone in the Boston basin. With a million thoughts spinning around in my mind, I waited for the starter's commands. Fully ready or not, post time was at hand. If we each committed to the race at hand, we could overcome any of the past month's obstacles. So we thought. Could the nine of us together do anything? We were about to find out.

As defending champions, we would have the privilege of crossing the line first. There would be open water ahead that was ours to attack. We got off the line well and settled into a strong pace. The second crew, Brown University, waited a full minute to cross the line, so we would have no possible way to judge our performance. Perhaps it was fitting that we raced against ourselves down the Charles that day because our biggest competition recently had been ourselves anyway.

Despite the usual crowds of drunkards, there were still plenty of fans intently watching. The hype of the U.S. versus the Dutch and the

Canadian/German composite had provided some excitement. The crowds were cheering loudly, and I remember hearing lots of screaming as we cranked down the river. We rushed past throngs of people whose cheers would die down quickly thanks to the speed of the shell. With each cheer of support, I could feel the intensity of the oarsmen. Each blade zipped through the water and propelled the boat closer to the finish line.

Midway through the race disaster struck. One of the oarsmen lost control of his blade. The edge stuck in the water and the handle jumped over his head. In front of several thousand fans along the shore, the supposedly best eight in the United States committed the most novice of mistakes. We were in a world of trouble. For a few precious moments, we came to dead stop. The guilty athlete quickly recovered and we drove the boat back up to speed.

During the few moments following the crab I did my best to allow the crew to regain its composure. In the back of each of our minds we thought that the race was lost. How could we possibly recover? But somehow we had to find our rhythm. I tried to remember Spracky's advice for this situation. "A crab is never as bad as it seems. Although it may seem like a tremendous loss, it really only costs you a few seconds. What matters is how you react to the crab, how quickly you regain your rhythm."

In our race, it took about three minutes to get that rhythm back. The guys pulled their guts out in those three minutes, but we did not do it exactly together. Instead, each man tried to do it himself. Then it just clicked. Someone yelled something and the boat was back on fire. We had a chance yet. There were still five or so minutes left, and we had to give it everything. Even then it might not be enough.

Our push to the finish line was strong, and the time on my watch appeared to be very fast. I thought we were within seconds of the course record. But the agony of head racing is that you have no idea how the competition fared. Maybe the Dutch had gotten into a crash back in the pack? Maybe they had a great row? We could do nothing but wait.

We returned to the Northeastern University boathouse to put the boat away, shower, change and head to the awards ceremony. In the locker room, our usually vocal crew was noticeably silent. No one wanted to imagine what would happen if we had blown the race. On the ride to the awards ceremony I ran into plenty of people I knew. Each one had his or her own inside scoop on the race results. One person said we won by nearly a minute. Another said we finished fourth. My stomach was doing flips in anticipation of the real results.

An hour after the race, the unofficial results were posted: United States first, Netherlands second by an enormous twenty three seconds, and the Canada/Germany composite crew fourth. Whew, relief! But then word came that the Dutch crew was protesting the results. In their opinion, there was a mistake in the official timing.

For another hour, the rumors went flying again. Yes, we had won. No, the Dutch protest was upheld and we lost. Finally, the ceremony concluded with the announcement of the winners of the Championship Eights. The speaker proclaimed, "New champions (my heart stopped) the United States."

As I strolled onto stage with my boat mates to receive my medal, I whispered in the announcer's ear, "We're not new champs, we're defending." And so we left for San Diego to begin the final chapter in our four-year odyssey.

Chapter 4: 1996

It didn't take long for tempers to flare in the 1996 season. From the very first training session, the scene on the water was more aggressive and more combative. People started to look at every workout as do-or-die. This all-too-early show of emotion symbolized the increased level of anxiety. The squad had endured tense times throughout the past three years, but everyone knew that this was the one year that really counted. You can be on every World Championship team for the past three years and have won medals every time; but in the eyes of the average American, those accomplishments pale in comparison to simply competing at a single Olympics.

Within a few days of arriving in San Diego, Mike asked for last summer's eight to come to the boathouse an hour early to discuss a few matters without the rest of the squad. We rehashed the Finland final for the first time as a group. Mike thought that we entered the race in great position to win, but we failed to produce the necessary commitment to cross the line first. He didn't question the crew's dedication to winning, but did question our commitment to the big push. "When you had the move, nothing happened. There was no commitment. It only takes one man to go soft and that feeling creeps through the rest of the crew." At that moment I felt as though my guts were ripped out of my stomach. I'd guess that I wasn't alone.

Strangely enough, the "shipwrecks" were never mentioned. After the meeting, some of the guys wondered if we should have brought them to Mike's attention. After our recent problems with crabs–two in Finland, one in Boston, and a few in training this summer—it seemed like a problem that needed to be addressed.

After a few other side issues, we began the whole squad meeting. As in years past, Mike discussed the basic tenets of day-to-day training: priority to top athletes, the advantages of training in a pack, and so on. Despite the usual subjects, you could sense a tougher tone in this lecture. That undercurrent was directly related to the arrival of the Olympic year. The message was clear—the past years have been good, but this year we've got to step it up. We'll get only one chance to get it right in Atlanta, and we can't miss a step en route to the middle of the Olympic medal dock. The message on the first week's training program summed it up nicely, "When you take one step towards a major goal, you are already successful."

The first few months of training for the 1996 season were relatively uneventful. The days were long and grueling. Mike consistently pushed the oarsmen through incredibly tough workouts. While three workouts per day used to seem tough, he added a fourth weight session a couple of nights per week to make life that much harder.

To make life even tougher, we also engaged in a variety of training sessions to prepare for the expected heat in Atlanta. On a few occasions, we traveled to San Diego State's athlete physiology department, where the guys would row on ergometers inside a heat chamber designed to simulate extreme temperatures and humidity. Even worse than the heat chamber, though, were the workouts where Spracky required guys to wear extra layers of clothing (like sweatshirts and tights) while rowing in the California heat. If workouts weren't tough enough already, the heat preparation practices were absolute murder.

On a daily basis, guys would come home to pass out on the couch. By the end of the week, they were lucky to have the energy to stay up late enough to have a beer or two. Saturdays they were content to do virtually nothing but conserve their energy to prepare for the next week. Since my body wasn't racked with pain, I could only sympathize with the physical sacrifices oarsmen made on a daily basis. Undoubtedly, the guys were on their way to the best shape of their lives.

There was one other notable difference for the 1996 season. Silken Laumann, the Canadian women's single sculler, would be joining our training group permanently. Silken had rowed for Spracky in Canada through Barcelona, and she had worked with him intermittently since then. In fact, we all knew Silken pretty well since she had joined us in Oberageri the previous summer. Now, though, Silken wanted Mike to become her full-time coach once again with Atlanta just around the corner.

Silken is one of the amazing personalities in the international rowing community. After years of success, she was a strong favorite heading into the women's single sculls competition in Barcelona in 1992 when tragedy struck. Just months before the Olympics, she was involved in a freak boating accident when she crashed with the German men's pair in a world cup race in Essen, Germany. The German boat actually pierced her leg and she suffered a nasty injury. She could not walk for weeks, but she trained as hard as possible in a boat and on a rowing machine. Miraculously, she was able to compete in Barcelona, where she captured a bronze medal in a heroic performance. Canada rallied around her story, and she became a national celebrity. In fact, her story probably overshadowed the Canadian men's eight's gold medal performance.

Silken moved to San Diego to train with our crew with her husband John Wallace, who was a superb rower in his own right. John stroked Spracky's eight in Canada for three years until he was moved to bow as a member of the Olympic champion crew. Both Silken and John were great additions to our training group. They had each enjoyed tremendous success in rowing and had both survived an Olympics with Mike. Whenever we had no idea what Mike was thinking, it was a safe bet that John and Silken had the answer.

Saturday February 10, 1996   *Chula Vista, CA*

Hard to believe that selection is just around the corner. Already everyone has got their shorts in a bundle. After all, this year isn't just another selection process. For most guys, this is the FINAL selection process of their careers. No more tomorrow. My guess is still that the eight will be largely the same. The only potential change at this point is Ted Murphy in for Jeff Klepacki. Jeff sets a great rhythm, but he hasn't been competitive enough otherwise. Ted is the erg king and rowing continually well in the pairs. The starboard gray area is a little more muddled, but I would not be surprised to see the same four guys as last year in there. We'll see.

Two other developments to report. One veteran is on his way out, while another is on his way in. Chip McKibben left camp permanently after being diagnosed with Epstein-Barr disease, also known as chronic fatigue syndrome. The virus attacks elite athletes in the midst of heavy training and leaves them without enough energy to get through a normal day without exercise. Chip has fought hard to get back his training strength, but has never been able to return to earlier seasons' performance levels. It is very sad to watch a friend lose this fight.

On the other hand, Doug Burden has arrived in camp and is fighting for an Olympic seat. Doug is a two-time Olympian who won a bronze medal with the U.S. eight in 1988 in Seoul and a silver medal with the U.S. straight four in 1992 in Barcelona. Although he has taken a lot of grief for showing up late in the process, his actions on the water speak louder than words. Doug is a very skilled oarsman and he obviously knows what it takes to win.

Personally, I feel like I am performing okay. It is always hard to say at this time of year since coxswains are used so sparingly. We row the eights one to three times per week, which does not really give you a good feel of things. The only two coxswains in camp are me and Pete Cipollone. Pete and I have faced off for several years now, and I have bested him each time.

Nevertheless, I am focused on the future, not the past. Every time I am in there I try to assert myself, not only as the best coxswain on Lake Otay, but as the best coxswain I can be. My primary motivation is to improve every day, to give my absolute best every day. If I can achieve those goals I can be the U.S. coxswain in the Olympics and help to bring home that medal (the right one of course).

During an innocuous team meeting in mid-February, Spracky made a rare verbal slip that caused me a bit of brief joy and then an extended heartache. When addressing the whole squad, Spracky mentioned that Pete Cipollone would accompany a group of small boats to Europe while the eight was in San Diego. Because Pete and I were the only two coxes, this statement logically meant that I would cox the eight. Little did I know that Spracklen's abruptness would work badly against me. The oarsmen were about to enter into the most stressful selection period of their careers. They would be damned if they would let the coxswain selection fall harmlessly to the side.

Within a few days of Spracky's misstatement one of the oarsmen asked Spracky if he intended to end cox selection before it started. At that point, Spracky realized his error and let the guys know that this was not the case. By that same afternoon Spracky calmly informed me that the game was not over. I wanted to be ready.

Monday February 19, 1996   *San Diego, CA*

For the past months, I may have gotten a little too comfortable. I have let myself get too happy, too pleased with where I am now. There are less than six months until the men's eight Olympic Final in Atlanta on July 28, 1996–160 days to be exact. I have got to get a ton more fired up, more focused, and more determined. The time for happily pursuing this goal is over. I have 160 days left in my international rowing career, and I need to make each one count. If we are going to win that gold medal on the twenty-eighth, each man has to be ready to sacrifice anything and everything for the moment. I have no control over what the other eight guys do, but I can damn well get my own head in the game.

Maybe this sounds a little silly, but who cares? It does not matter what anyone thinks. What matters is that I stay true to my character. What matters is that we win that race.

While running today, I worked myself into some kind of runner's high. The pace was so quick that I let my mind wander a little. In a moment of clarity, I realized that I had to shelve any of my doubts, any of my fears, anything except an intense desire and commitment to winning the Olympics. I want to sit on the line on the twenty-eighth and know that I am absolutely prepared to win. I want to be more ready than Jeroen Duysten (cox from the Netherlands), more ready than Peter Thiedes (cox from Germany), more ready than Gheorghe Marin (cox from Romania). More ready than anyone in the world. Nothing else matters. Those five and a half minutes are it.

Selection for the 1996 Olympic eight began in early March. As usual, the process began with a time trial in pairs. Don and Fred walked away with a victory, which pretty much guaranteed them seats in the eight. The rest of the results were all over the place. The second place crew consisted of Porter Collins and Ted Murphy, two young, powerful guys who made a strong case for seats in the eight. Meanwhile, Jon Brown and Mike Peterson stumbled badly and their pair finished a very disappointing eighth. Understandably, JB was beside himself. His hopes to rejoin the eight seemed to be disappearing. In the days before the next stage of selection, I sent him the following email for support:

"*Your situation has been on my mind, and I wanted to send you a few thoughts. Please pardon me if I'm a bit on the harsh side, or unorganized for that matter. I just want to write down some ideas and pass them along.*

"*Watching you row today, I can tell your mind is elsewhere. I can only imagine the millions of thoughts going through your mind, so it is understandable. Today it was okay to still be in shock, so to speak. Now you have to get that out of your system. You get tomorrow to rest, a bit of training on Sunday, and then the five minute shot on Monday.*

"*My best advice for preparation for that piece, and the subsequent pieces, is to re-focus all your energy, all your thoughts on yourself. I know it feels like the world is crashing around you. You have probably thought a lot about all the people you think are counting on you to be in Atlanta. Let me remind you that you are doing this for one person—yourself. Fuck everyone else. It's your goddamned medal, not theirs. You train for it, you earn it, and you get to keep it. Who gives a shit what other people think of you? What matters is that you can look in the mirror and be proud of yourself at the end of the day. It may seem strange to think so selfishly, but that is the fact.*

"*One thing that also sucks about selection is the loneliness. In a high pressure race at least you can share the burden with other teammates. Now you are alone. Try to use that power of your self, your individuality as a strength rather than a weakness. You have proven yourself time and again in the past three years as a stalwart member of the U.S. eight. That boat would not have enjoyed its success were it not for your efforts. Don't fucking forget that.*

"*When you line-up on Monday keep that laser beam focus. It does not matter what else is going on around you. No one else's thoughts or actions make a goddamned difference except your own. If Jon Brown performs to potential that four will move. Stay long, keep attacking and be positive.*

"*Best,*
Steven"

Selection proceeded in a convoluted, unexpected manner. But then again, after the craziness we had seen in years past, what was normal? A few days after the pairs time trial, Spracky held races in straight fours to sort guys out further. And for the final step of the eight selection, we moved into the eight and tested out several line-ups. Six seats were set: Porter Collins, Fred Honebein, Bob Kaehler, Jamie Koven, Ted Murphy and Don Smith. Jon Brown and Jeff Klepacki would battle it out for the last port seat, while Doug Burden, Sean Hall and Mike Peterson fought for the last starboard seat. After another set of trials, Jon Brown and Doug Burden joined the eight. Without Jeff to stroke the boat, Spracky decided to try JB in the stroke seat.

While these eight guys celebrated the real battle for survival began. There were a lot of solid oarsmen left out of the eight and now just a precious few seats left for Atlanta. After a few more days of highly stressful trials, the final line-ups were chosen. The four included Jeff Klepacki, Sean Hall, Tom Murray and Jason Scott, while the straight pair would be Adam Holland and Mike Peterson. All crews still had to win the official Olympic trials, but no one expected any serious threats. These line-ups were not set in stone for Olympic competition, but history had shown that Spracky was averse to shaking things up too much. The only seat left for selection was the coxswain.

Tuesday March 12, 1996   *Chula Vista, CA*

Today I asked Mike what coxswain selection would entail. I further commented that I wanted a chance to earn my seat in the boat like everyone else. Let the oarsmen choose whom they think is best. That may sound a bit cocky or arrogant for me to bring up, but I had my reasons. I wanted Mike to know that I am not afraid of putting my ability on the line. If the guys in the eight think that Pete is better than I, then so be it. Obviously, I have the confidence in my abilities to lay it on the line and be judged.

The next few days could be very uncomfortable. The guys selected for the eight have already started some of their celebrations. You could tell by their behavior on the water in tonight's eight practice and in the locker room afterwards. They are psyched as hell, and they have every right to be. I find myself in no-man's land. I want to seem positive about the year ahead, but careful not to be too happy because I am not one of the crew yet.

It hurts a little, but I guess I should suffer like everyone else. The worst part is this waiting game. In 1993, there was at least a full week before the coxswain situation was settled. I need to be mentally ready to face any obstacle. I have worked too long and too hard for that seat to let ANYONE stand in my way. I will not be denied.

I had no idea about the nightmare that lay ahead for me. My sense of what was going to happen was completely off. My own selection process would be the most difficult time of my four seasons with the squad. When I watched JB endure his near tragedy I felt that I understood the pain he felt. No way.

Coxswain selection started off innocently enough. Spracky announced that Pete would have the boat Monday, Tuesday and Wednesday, whereas I would get it Thursday and Friday. On Friday afternoon the eight would sit down with Spracky and make their final pick. Heading into the process I felt nervous, but mostly excited that I could prove myself and get this over with.

Tuesday March 19, 1996   *Chula Vista, CA*

Some strange feelings this week. For one thing, I am unaccustomed to being on the outside looking in at the eight. During these past three years, I have been involved with every possible aspect of that crew's development—training, racing, boat meetings, selection, and so on. To sit idly by and watch the boat progress without taking part is gut-wrenching. This part of the process makes me feel absolutely awful. I can see the eight oarsmen walking around, knowing they are Olympians and having a ball. Yet, I am on the periphery of that group.

At the same time, this "outsider" feeling makes me that much more motivated to get back in the boat. I yearn for my chance to sit in the stern, steer the boat like an arrow, and nail every call. I am not afraid to lay my soul on the line and show those guys what I can do. With the confidence of three full seasons experience in my back pocket, I know I can do the job well. Now I want the chance to do it even better.

I guess what it comes down to is just worrying about yourself. All I can do is my very best. I have no control over Pete's performance, so why think about it? When I get in the boat on Thursday and Friday morning for my chances, I am going to cox to the best of my abilities. Then let the chips fall where they may.

As the week wore on things seemed to be going my way. During his time in the eight Pete made a few unfortunate errors, including telling the crew to paddle before the finish line in an important time trial, a cardinal sin for a cox. Meanwhile, during my two days in the boat everything was fine. I'm not sure that my coxing was all-world, but I felt that I had done my best and performed solidly.

On the day scheduled for cox selection, after a forty-five minute meeting, the guys and Spracky emerged from the back room in the boathouse and announced that they needed more time to make a decision. Because they had never experienced Pete in a race situation, they wanted to use Pete in next weekend's San Diego Crew Classic. I was floored.

It took every ounce of composure I had not to burst into tears. I was flabbergasted at this turn of events and didn't know what to do next. My world was crashing around me. Suddenly, the years of work I had devoted to the Atlanta Olympics seemed to be wasted. My life-long dream was in jeopardy, not to mention the hopes and expectations of all my family and friends.

Saturday March 23, 1996   *Chula Vista, CA*

Woke up a couple of times during the night and wondered if yesterday actually happened. Is my world crashing around me or was I dreaming? Unfortunately, it really did happen, and I have to live with it.

I have been speaking with as many guys as possible to try to figure out what's going on. Everybody told me not to worry, stay cool and keep my head. The guys in the four (Jeff, Sean, Tom and Jason) each expressed disbelief. They figured that the guys in the eight want me to bust my ass and feel the heat as badly as they did to make the boat.

Another common theme of advice last night was that I was definitely the better cox. Not one guy even hinted that Pete could hold a candle to my performance on the water. Which brings me to the question at the heart of this issue, why?

I guess I can understand the idea of making me bust my ass for the seat. Somehow that is what I thought last week was all about—Pete was in the boat for three days, I was in it for two days, then decision time. The decision they have come to about the Crew Classic seems a bit cruel. Part of me wonders if they are abusing their power to punish me in some way for being Spracky's right hand man. The core oarsmen are picked right away without much consideration. I guess that I falsely assumed that I, too, was a core member of the boat. I cannot believe that no one went to bat for me in the meeting. I cannot believe that the majority of those oarsmen would rather go to the line with Pete than with me.

There is no doubt that the next eight days are going to be some of the longest of my life. I will probably only cox the boat a few times, including the 1500m pieces on Monday. Those will definitely be my big chance to show my stuff. I have to take a stand and show that I can handle the pressure. I am simply at a loss over how to act and what to say. I guess the best thing is just to be natural, to be myself.

The week of waiting trudged forward terribly slowly. Because the eight wanted more exposure to Pete, I played a limited role in the boat. For the most part, I rode in the launch and watched impatiently. Meanwhile, I stubbornly encouraged family and friends to leave me alone. As far as I was concerned, no one outside San Diego could help me now, so I'd just as soon go it alone. To try to pass some of the time I bought the latest one thousand-page biography of George Patton hoping for courage. In the book Patton was quoted as saying "No sacrifice is too great if you can attain an end." I hoped he was right.

Time eventually did pass by, as did the San Diego Crew Classic. In their race, the eight beat a Canadian crew by a decent margin. From the shore it was hard to tell how things went. That night all I could do was try to stay calm and keep a positive attitude.

Sunday March 31, 1996   *San Diego, CA*

Feeling pretty good this evening. A number of things happened today to give me a lot of positive vibes for the big decision. I am at ease with myself and hopeful that this will all work out for the best.

As much as I dreaded the horror of going down to the course and watching the eight race without me, it wasn't that bad. I spent most of the day in the Steward's Enclosure with Spracky and his wife Annie. She is a wonderful woman who has been like a den mother to our crew for three years.

Not long after we sat down, Annie said to me, "Who would have ever thought this would happen, Steve? Another cox, what a bit of bad business. Don't worry though, I know you'll make it. I want you to make it so badly, and I know that Mike does, too. He told me so. And if he has anything to say about it, you'll be in. But don't worry, it won't even come to that. I know you'll be in there. I just know it."

It was very touching of her to say those things to me and it meant a lot. She put me at ease and re-invigorated my confidence. I set out for the rest of the day to show everyone that I could hold my head up high in the face of danger.

Spracky waited two days until after the San Diego Crew Classic to call the official meeting for coxswain selection. As usual, Spracky wanted emotions to subside as much as possible before making a big decision. Then finally it was done.

Tuesday April 2, 1996   *Chula Vista, CA*

It has been one hell of a long day. After a half an hour of closed door talks Mike came back to fetch Pete and me out of the office. We briskly walked back into the video room at the boathouse.

When we sat down to hear the dreaded news, I remember clutching Patton's book tightly to my body. As I sat down on the couch I was thinking to myself, "I'm going to get it. I know it's going to be me. They only talked for half an hour. No way that was long enough to kick me out. I'm gonna get this thing."

Mike opened by saying, 'Steven is going to cox the eight." There was an abrupt silence that permeated to open room.

Pete kindly leaned over and said, "Hey. Congratulations, man."

I looked up to the ceiling and pulled the book tighter to my body. I thought to myself, "Thank God. Thank God. I made it. I'm going to Atlanta. Thank God."

Mike continued, "It was a dreadful process and this is the way we are going." Then a long silence. For maybe a full minute, we just sat there and let the news sink in. Selection was done. Mike spoke for a little more and explained the decision. "I told the guys that unless there was something decisive, unless it was overwhelming, I am going to choose Steven. He has three years experience, and I have confidence in his abilities. And that is what you have going against you Peter, three years of experience. Steven has been through all of these trials before and knows how it all works. You should both know that all the feedback about both of you was positive. There was no one against anyone. I was actually surprised."

There was little else said. The room was eerily quiet. As I got up to leave Pete also stood. He said, "Congratulations again, Steve. You deserve it." We shook hands and he then gave me a hug. Very touching scene that took me aback some due to its heaviness. When all is said and done, Pete is a solid guy. He'll get his day.

I walked to the office trying to keep my head down and act as humbly as possible. I grabbed the phone and made two quick calls. First was to Dad, who broke down crying during our conversation. Needless to say he was overwhelmed with the emotion of the moment. I was just happy it was over. We spoke for a few minutes though, and he continued to tell me how proud he was. Next I called my girlfriend (and now wife) who had stood by me through the whole process. She was equally relieved

The rest of the day has been a whirlwind of congratulations, phone calls and e-mails. I wanted to write back to everyone who showed their support during these trying weeks. Wonderful feeling, but exhausting too.

I'm going to be an Olympian—a dream realized today.

Thursday April 4, 1996   *Chula Vista, CA*

Two days after realizing one of my life-long dreams, the reality is slowly setting in. Every few hours, I think about how cool it is that I am going to Atlanta. I want to be humble about it, but another part of me wants to stamp "Olympian" on my forehead. For so long I have thought,

"If…maybe…possibly…" Now, it is all reality. I'm going to the Olympics.
All of my greatest dreams are going to come true. I can't wait.

Coxswain selection was a stressful time, but once I joined the Olympic eight life got even more hectic. The Olympic Games were several months away, but our schedule made time fly. Between selection and the Olympic competition we would go to Atlanta for the official Olympic Trials, back to San Diego for training, up to Seattle for a publicity trip, over to Europe for racing experience, back to San Diego again, and finally off to Georgia where we would train for two weeks before heading into the big event.

Our first trip as a crew was to the U.S. Olympic Trials in Atlanta at the official Olympic site in Gainesville. Every Olympic event was open to challenge, but only the small boats would face any real competition. This made for a very strange situation. The trip was a formality for half of the trials participants. People rowing in bigger boats (eights and fours) went to Atlanta for an easy paddle and a fun trip. Meanwhile, people in the smaller boats were fighting tooth and nail to earn their stripes as American Olympians.

We went to Atlanta for less than one week, took care of business and then left. At last it was official. I was an Olympian.

In our brief return to San Diego, we began to experience the growing hype for the Olympics. In addition to the daily media barrage pointing toward Atlanta, we experienced some of the magic first-hand. The Olympic torch had just arrived in the United States, and one of its first stops was San Diego. Someone had arranged for us to row the torch across Lake Otay for the media. Each member of every boat training in San Diego held the torch, and I got to carry it while the boat paddled from one end of the lake to the other. Seeing the symbolic flame in my own hands was just another reminder that the big race was drawing near.

While the Olympic hoopla grew, our boat began to develop. During training the character of the crew took shape. The trouble was that you could never quite tell how fast we would be. Some days we would be blazing fast and perform record times. Other days the boat seemed flat and lacked the spark to get anyone excited. The challenge ahead was to perform consistently at a high level.

Our schedule called for one quick trip to Germany for racing experience. We would row in a tune-up race in Mannheim and then compete in the infamous Thyssen Cup in Duisburg against everyone we could expect to face in Atlanta. The simple goal of our European tour was to return to San Diego knowing that we could win in Atlanta. The operative word was "could." So long as we had confidence that we could beat everyone that was enough to be ready for the Olympic Games. The tune-up race in Mannheim went very well. In a race against mixed competition we crushed the field and set a course record. For the first time since formation we all felt like we were on a solid course to victory in Atlanta. What we learned in Duisburg, though, was that we had a long way to go.

As usual, Duisburg was set up as two one-day regattas. We would race in heats each morning and finals each afternoon. Of course, the race that mattered most was the final on Sunday. Compared to past regattas, I could never have imagined that we would experience such a range of emotion in forty-eight hours.

On Saturday the regatta started off fine. We were edged out by Romania in our heat, but easily qualified for the afternoon final. In the final our problems began. In a race with a raging tailwind, we stumbled down the course and finished dead last in a field of six. The mood of the crew afterward was one of disappointment to say the least. Now we had one more day of racing to pull our heads out of our asses before we boarded the plane for home.

Sunday morning's heat didn't go too much better. We rowed well enough to qualify for the afternoon final, but we were beaten by a rejuvenated Canadian crew who was all too happy to shut us down.

Heading into the afternoon final the pervasive emotion was confusion. How could we be so fast one minute and so average the next? We all hoped like hell that the fast crew would show up that afternoon.

In my fourth consecutive Thyssen Cup we rowed a pretty solid race. We didn't set the world on fire, nor did we fall on our faces. We managed to place third in a tight race–2.2 seconds behind the Netherlands (who had won every race they had entered that year and were now odds-on favorites to win in Atlanta), 0.4 seconds behind Romania, 0.6 seconds ahead of Canada, and substantially ahead of Germany and Australia who trailed the field.

Before leaving the course that day I had a curious conversation with a friend of mine from the British Olympic Team, Miriam Batten, who was familiar with Spracky's coaching style. She said, "I don't think Spracky wanted you to win early. The word on Americans is that if they win early they get big heads. Now he can build you up for the big finish in Atlanta." Hopefully, after six weeks of rebuilding under Spracky's psychological care we would be ready to win. Upon returning to San Diego we certainly had a lot of work to do.

After our only international racing prior to the Olympics, we returned to San Diego for seven crucial weeks of training. Our next, and final, trip would be to Georgia for the last stage of preparation before the Summer Olympic Games. The ensuing weeks were filled with emotion. The pressure of the impending race of our lives was just around the corner and we all had to deal with those expectations on a daily basis.

As is his style, Spracky concocted test after test to challenge each of us to perform up to an acceptable standard. Mike specifically threatened to make a change in the crews between the eight and the four. The theory was that the eight was inconsistent because it lacked the steady, attacking rhythm provided by Jeff Klepacki. This threat forced all the ports to worry about job security. In my case, Spracky scrutinized my steering and calls more than ever before. As a crew, we did time trials bi-weekly to specifically analyze our progress, or lack thereof. Time was growing short, and the mood was tense.

Saturday May 25, 1996   **San Diego, CA**

This week is not going to be pretty. We had a couple of days off to relax from jet-lag on Tuesday and Wednesday. We started rowing again on Thursday, and Mike wasted little time setting the record straight. After a brief steady state row in the morning, we met in the afternoon to discuss the results of our trip. Never do I remember a meeting so blunt or so harsh.

The gist of Mike's speech was that we were not close enough on target to winning in Atlanta. He repeated the fact that the goal of our racing in Europe was to leave Duisburg knowing we could win in Atlanta. The mentality of the athlete, he argued, was "Yeah, we can win. I know we can do it…." In reality, though, he feels that we are not flowing together. Despite having stronger guys, more powerful erg results, more intense training, and the best of everything in the program, something is not flowing. We had a "one-off" in Mannheim, but otherwise, we have not showcased the speed we should on a daily basis.

Mike's rant went on for some time, probably upwards of twenty minutes. Another allegation he made was that the 1995 eight was certainly faster than this crew. In 1995, we could gain a half-length on the field at the start. In 1996, our one minute push is non-existent. So what is the difference? "Should we try Jeff Klepacki at stroke?" Mike asked. You could feel the tension mounting in the room.

The overwhelming response from all of us was that something needed to change. No one is pointing the finger at anyone specifically, but we all recognize that something has to change if we are going to bring home the gold in Atlanta. Maybe Jeff should return to stroke and JB back to six. It's impossible to guess what might happen, but it has to be something.

Since that fateful meeting two days ago, it feels as though a death knell has settled over the group. Usually, we are a fun-loving bunch of guys who screw around a bit. Now there is the hint of panic in the air. We had all planned on being in the hunt for the gold medal at the Olympics. Before the racing in Duisburg one week ago this afternoon, no one would have told you differently. Now our world is spinning. We all want to do whatever it takes to get the ship going in the right direction again. The million dollar question is–What should we be doing differently? What should I be doing differently? I'll be damned if I know.

Talking it over with Spracky yesterday gave me a different perspective. We discussed the idea of a crew's expectations versus reality, and how that influences psychology. We went into Duisburg thinking we could win, maybe even dominate. When we rowed terribly and finished sixth on Saturday, our confidence went right down the tubes. We saved face by finishing third on Sunday night, but still far off our expectations. As a result, our trip seems like a potential disaster. On the other hand, if we had gone to Germany hoping to be in the middle of the pack, we would have come home happy.

We have been in the thick of the battle for each world championship for three years. After a year of incredibly hard training, we all envisioned that this would be the year to put the U.S. back on the top of the rowing world. We wanted to be the ones to re-claim U.S. supremacy in the Olympic eight. Suddenly, that dream seems like a far away prayer.

I am definitely feeling the increased pressures circling around me. Everyone's hopes and dreams rest on my performance– friends, family, etc. Upwards of one hundred of my family and friends are making the trip to the Olympics to watch me compete. Before Duisburg, there was never any doubt in my mind we would be fighting for the win. Now I wonder if we'll be fighting to be in the final. It makes me sick.

I guess it comes back to your own mind. If I have the mindset that we're in the middle of the pack then that's where we'll finish. If we fight and grind out some speed in the coming two months and regain our confidence,

then we can get back to the front of the pack. The good news is that we were
only 2.2 seconds off the Dutch. It's not like those guys are untouchable. They
have been on a hot streak, whereas we have been on a downward spiral. We
need to rise from the depths and come out swinging like true champions. No
second chances this time. No next year. It's all or nothing in Atlanta.

When training resumed we didn't have time to sit around and feel
sorry for ourselves. We had work to do, and we had to do it quickly. For
the first couple of weeks we got back to basics. We rowed three times per
day and went for long steady-state rows. The focus was not on power,
but rather on establishing a solid, consistent and dependable rhythm.
Like the year before in Oberageri, the boat started to gel. Spirits began
to rise again.

Another crucial change at this time was a re-shuffling of the line-up.
Spracky moved Fred Honebein to stroke, Don Smith to seven, JB to six
and Jamie Koven to five. The bow four contained Ted Murphy in the
four seat, Porter Collins in three, Bob Kaehler in two and Doug Burden
in bow. This adjustment put the four guys who had been with Spracky
the longest in the stern four. Moreover, Fred and Don, who had consistently been the strongest pair for four years became the stern pair
(stroke and seven seat). Essentially, Spracky was calling upon our two
top oarsmen to lead us to victory in Atlanta.

Don and Fred were a great example of good boat chemistry. Prior to
rowing together, neither had achieved too much success at the national
team level. But in the pair they dominated everyone in the U.S. from
1993 through 1996. There wasn't anything special they did, they just
made the boat go fast.

Fred was not an incredibly vocal guy either on or off the water. In
fact, I'd describe him as a reluctant leader. Yet Fred was probably the
best athlete on the squad (in any sport), and the fact that he dominated
physically forced most people to look up to him. Fred wasn't thrilled to

stroke the eight, but he would do whatever it took to return our boat to proper form.

Don was sort of an enigma. There were sometimes that Don was incredibly intense, and other times that he was goofing around. He was very serious on the water about discipline and attitude in the boat, but off the water he was a huge wise-ass. Still, underneath his joking attitude, Don was fired up to win and excited to be called up to the seven seat to spark a flame in the crew.

Once we had put in a few weeks of long mileage, we returned to speed work and race-specific work. The crew continued to improve, and our performances in time trials showed that we were getting faster. Unfortunately for me, I began having trouble with one of the most essential coxing skills, steering. What made this situation more frustrating was that I had always thought of steering as one of my strongest skills.

In the month preceding the Olympics we switched back and forth between two types of boats–a German Empacher (the type of boat we had used every year so far) and a new American boat called a Resolute. Each company wanted us to use their boat, and they produced sleeker boat designs to argue that they had a better product. In terms of hydro-dynamics, one way to make a boat faster is to reduce the drag on the rudder by cutting down the rudder's size. A direct result of these increasingly shrinking rudders was that racing shells were harder to steer. In fact, I learned at the Olympics that the German eight had decided not to use Empacher's newest design.

My steering problems could be blamed on a lot of things–a more sensitive rudder, changing boats daily or simply mental stress. Regardless of the source of the problem, Spracky noticed my mistakes and readily pointed them out. Although I had heard Spracky pick on oarsmen hundreds of times, I had never personally experienced his venom. It was not pretty. One day he called out to me, "It's going to be pretty sad if the whole world watches on TV as you go from buoy to buoy and we lose by two feet." Thanks Coach.

Despite my personal battle with steering the crew kept making positive strides. We won the time-trial two weeks in a row by comparing times with the smaller boats and Silken in her single. We had put in the necessary work in San Diego and were gearing up for the home stretch.

Friday June 28, 1996   *San Diego, CA*

I am beginning to feel the rush of excitement that comes with the rapid approach of race day. We are within a month now, and I find constant daily reminders that the big day will soon be at hand. Every time I see an Olympic advertisement or publicity of some kind, I feel a little chill in my bones. You can't look anywhere these days without hearing about the upcoming Olympics. Since the U.S. is the king of media hype, this could be the event of the year for our nation. I try to remind myself of the responsibility I carry as a representative of our country at the Games. I want to win so badly.

At least in the past there was always next year, next season, and another chance. After July 28th there won't be any second chances. We have to do it then. We have to win that damned race. Realistically, I won't be around in 2000 in Sydney, Australia. Even if I would, who could say what chance the U.S. will have in four years?

The fact is that right now our boat is flying. We may not be the favorites in Atlanta, but that's just fine. Let everyone think that the Dutch are the ones to beat. That will take the extra pressure off our crew and allow us to remain focused as a unit. Now we have something to prove. The extra incentive to prove everyone wrong is a powerful ally.

I still have the same dream. I have dreamed of winning in Atlanta for four years. Even before I saw the venue, I could picture what it would be like to climb to the top of the medal podium there. After racing there a few times, I can now put some pictures to my dreams—the angle of the sun, the position of the stands, the feel of the water, and so on. I can see it all before me now.

I want to win so desperately that I won't let anything stand in my way. When the whole ordeal is over on July 28th I don't want any regrets. I have to walk away from that last race with my head high because I'm not going to have the chance to make amends.

The Olympic eight joking around after our last training session in San Diego. From left to right: Steven Segaloff, Bob Kaehler, Ted Murphy, Porter Collins, Jamie Koven, Jon Brown, Don Smith, Fred Honebein and Doug Burden.

Sunday July 7, 1996   *San Diego–Atlanta*

This is the trip I have waited a lifetime to take. United Flight #262 to Chicago, then Flight #1220 to Atlanta. I am aboard this plane as a member of the 1996 U.S. Olympic Team en route to competition at the Summer Games.

At this moment I am filled with a variety of emotions—joy, sadness, fear, excitement, and hunger to name a few. Our final days in San Diego were rather hectic. I won't be returning until mid-September, so there was a lot to organize. Now aboard the plane, I am looking forward to our final three weeks. It's going to be over before you know it. Gotta utilize every second to prepare for the big one.

Tomorrow, particularly, is a long awaited day. I have heard about the infamous Olympic outfitting process for many years. Compared to all the bits of gear we've ever received, tomorrow is the mother lode. For the past three years, I have been too superstitious to wear the Olympic rings. Tomorrow, I will get enough clothes emblazoned with the rings to last a lifetime. It should fulfill all of my wildest dreams.

One last note before a nap. We had a wonderful send-off party at the Eastlake Community Center Friday night hosted by Annie Spracklen. Amongst the 100-odd guests were all the people who helped during our three years as part of the San Diego community. There was a lot of emotion in the air as we all fed off the energy of the crowd. I kept thinking to myself, "Try to win for these people. Try to win for your country. They deserve your best."

At one point, we were each asked to say something to the crowd. Guys spoke as eloquently as I have ever heard. When Fred got up there, he lost it and broke down in tears. This only symbolized how deeply each of us feels a commitment to win for others.

I am trying to keep my head with all these emotions swirling about. Three weeks from this moment my rowing career will be over. Judgment will have passed, and the 1996 Olympic Champions will be crowned. I have dreamed of winning that medal for longer than I can remember. As the day approaches, I have to rise above the everyday distractions. I have the ability to contribute to a crew that could be the best. I am ready to showcase that talent.

Our initial experience in Atlanta was more incredible than I had imagined. Upon landing at Hartsfield Airport, we were whisked off to an airport hangar where we received our official athlete credentials. In the weeks that followed, these badges gave us access to virtually any-where in Atlanta. Credentials in hand, we were taken to the Olympic Village. We only spent two nights in the village before competition–one night upon arrival and a second night after opening ceremonies. The rest of the time we would spend either training a few hours south of Atlanta in Forsyth, Georgia or at a specially rented house during Olympic competition. It's a good thing we would spend so little time in the village because it was very distracting.

The Atlanta Olympic Committee transformed the Georgia Tech campus into the 1996 Olympic Village. The accommodations weren't spectacular, but the atmosphere was electric. Once inside the heavily guarded gates, Georgia Tech had become a university for elite athletes from around the world. Besides seeing international athletic stars roaming the campus, the Olympic Village placed a premium on per-sonal service. Whether it was food, medical assistance, tickets, travel arrangements, or anything else, you only had to ask and your wish was granted. On our second day in Atlanta the trend continued as we enjoyed the thrill of athlete processing.

Athlete processing is the formal procedure each American Olympian enjoys prior to competing in the Games. We were taken to a nearby Atlanta hotel, where we began our day with a videotaped greeting from President Clinton congratulating us on our selection to the U.S. Olympic team. Next, each athlete was given a large shopping cart to collect his or her loot. Imagine shopping at a giant department store, where everything is free and a tailor awaits to alter special items to your size immediately. In a few hours we acquired more gear than I knew what to do with–hats, shirts, shorts, sweaters, socks, sneakers, a leather jacket, a ring, an outfit for opening ceremonies and so on. Then we moved into the corporate area, where official team sponsors loaded us up with more stuff–a Motorola pager, an invitation to Busch Gardens Williamsburg after the Games and the filming of a McDonald's commer-cial to air in your hometown. Once we collected everything, a volunteer took all of our stuff and packed it into Olympic luggage. My head was spinning with excitement when I boarded the bus that took us back to training camp.

Before returning to Atlanta for Olympic competition we had a ten-day training camp in the small town of Forsyth, Georgia. Albeit a few hours away from Atlanta, this town had a big case of Olympic fever and they were thrilled to lavish us with attention. In our short stay we enjoyed a police escort to and from each practice, a town barbecue/autograph session and constant southern charm.

Meanwhile, back in the boat we were fine tuning for the racing ahead. Training was going well, and the crew seemed to be gaining speed. We began implementing strategic moves for racing and confidence was on the rise. Whereas in the past we had focused upon the start as our spot in the race to take control, for the Olympics we were more focused on the middle of the course. We felt that we were in superior physical condition and that we could take control through the guts of the race. Upon our return to Atlanta, we thought that we had a shot to win the gold medal after all.

Wednesday July 17, 1996   *Gainesville, GA*

This afternoon it finally hit me that we're here for the Olympics. Tonight we walked around the venue at the lake. Even though we have raced here twice before, the site is dramatically different. The most noticeable change is the 18,000 capacity grandstand on the other side of the lake. All seats are sold out for racing. Equally jaw-dropping is the proliferation of tents in the athlete's area. This place is wild.

I had a very familiar feeling while strolling through the rowing venue tonight, the same vibes as our evening walk along the banks of the River Thames at our first Henley Regatta in 1994. In those moments, I remember looking out on a quiet stretch of water that was soon to be filled with loud, raucous fans. I remember thinking that amidst all the races of the regatta, the big show was the Grand Challenge Cup for men's eights. Tonight, I had the same eerie feeling about thousands of fans going bonkers. Here at the Olympic Games, no race will be more closely watched than the final of the men's eights. And no boat will have more support than our American eight. This is what it's all about.

Ironically, the housing set up here in Gainesville is quite similar to Henley. USRowing has rented out a massive house, which holds the eight, four, Spracky and some personnel in the main house. The pair, the single, and assistant coaches are next door in the carriage house. Deceptively small from the outside, the house extends well back into a big yard and below ground level to a basement.

If it's amenities you want, we've got 'em—satellite dish TV, swimming pool, masseur, cooks, doctors, and plenty more. If there is anything we want or need, we will get it. The treatment is golden, so let's hope our performance is too.

The rowing lately has been going well. We did a few intense, timed pieces over the last two days with pretty good results. We posted a solid time in our final trial in Forsyth, but were outdone comparatively by two other boats. This morning was our chance for atonement. We did two more timed pieces and showed some blazing speed.

What was the difference? Amazingly, we weren't even at full strength today. Don pulled his back, so he sat out, Doug moved to seven, and Jim Neil (spare) went to bow. Even without one of our top guys, we crushed the pieces. JB believes, and I agree, that Spracky's aggressive talk before today's row had a profound effect. Basically, Spracky challenged us to go faster. He thought our performance yesterday was okay, but we were capable of much more. He is certainly right in keeping our egos in check. We cannot go to the line thinking we have got the race won. It was the death of us in Finland, and we can't make such a monumental mistake again.

Friday July 19, 1996   *Gainesville, GA*

Today is going to be an incredibly busy day. Here's our schedule:

5:40am	Wake up
6am	Leave for course
6:30am	8k Pre-Race practice
8am	Breakfast
8:30am	Return to house

Squeeze in a run, as long as possible

(9am	Regatta Draw)
10am	Leave for course
10:30am	Race Warm Up, then Two Timed Pieces (Each 750m)
12pm	Shower/Lunch
1pm	Leave for Olympic Village
2-4pm	Enjoy village
4pm	Nike apparel distribution
5-7pm	More village, Dinner
7pm	Leave for Opening Ceremony
2am (est.)	Return to village

Even amidst this busy schedule, plenty of other things were going on. In the draw, we learned that our heat would include Germany, Italy, Romania and Russia, with one to qualify for the final. It was good news that we didn't draw the Dutch who had dominated throughout the season. However, between Germany, Romania, Russia and ourselves, our heat contained four of the top five from last year's World Championships.

The other notable experience this day was the media attention that began to grow. After years of very mild media exposure, the press turned up the heat in Atlanta. Never before had I walked out of practice to find microphones thrust in my face as reporters from major newspapers and magazines fired off questions. Additionally, I was one of four members of the eight interviewed on camera by NBC for pre-race coverage. It was an absolute blast.

The U.S. Olympic eight prior to Opening Ceremonies in Atlanta. From left to right: Doug Burden, Bob Kaehler, Porter Collins, Ted Murphy, Steven Segaloff, Jamie Koven, Jon Brown, Don Smith, Fred Honebein and Mike Spracklen.

Saturday July 20, 1996   Olympic Village, GA

I might as well be living in a dream world. I am thankful to be leaving the Olympic Village in a few hours because there are simply too many distractions. I feel as though I've spent the past twenty four hours with my eyes wide open and my jaw on the floor. Our first race is about forty-eight hours from now, so it is time to shut everything out and focus.

Last night's opening ceremonies were a spectacle beyond words. Being a member of the American team walking into that stadium was nuts. No words could describe the mayhem.

The whole U.S. team gathered in the village to board the buses to the stadium. Just walking amongst our country's finest athletes was a big rush. Volunteers and spectators lined the roads clapping, cheering, and waving us on.

After a brief police-escort bus ride, we arrived at Fulton County Stadium, the home of the Atlanta Braves and next to the Olympic Stadium. Each country was seated in order of the parade of nations. The U.S.A., as host country, was last. Because we have such a large team, we enjoyed a couple of sections of the stadium. I walked around throughout the night and met tons of people–weightlifters, boxers, mountain bikers, beach volleyball players, fencers, divers, and so on. The only big-time stars I missed were the Dream Team. It was too crazy around them. A lot of the guys hung out with them because their extreme height gave them an extra advantage. At 5'4", I couldn't see anything more than five feet around me. In fact, I could barely make out Muhammad Ali lighting the torch because volleyball star Karch Kiraly blocked my view.

What was it like to feel, hear, and see the reaction of the crowd? 85,000 plus were screaming their heads off for the home team. It was truly insane. While I walked down the carpeted ramp, I had my oversized Panama hat in one hand and the other proudly waved an American flag. Throughout our victory lap, I was determined to live it up. I wanted to let it all hang out. Every step of the way, I tried to rile up the crowd, to soak in their energy. (I don't need to eat for the rest of the week now.) Patriotic tunes played in the background, cameras flashed, fingers raised the #1 sign–absolutely incredible. I want to document this all now. Although it is a feeling I'll never forget, the words to describe the moment do not come easily.

Sunday July 21, 1996   **Gainesville, GA**

I'm twenty-six years old today. In the midst of the Olympic hoopla, especially with our heat tomorrow, I am in a different zone. It's not that I don't appreciate my birthday. It just doesn't have the same feeling. There is so much excitement everywhere and we are so focused on our heat tomorrow that my birthday is truly an afterthought.

Today was the first day of competition. Even by 9am on a Sunday morning the stands were crowded. We left the course by 9:45am, and although it wasn't full, most seats were taken. I would bet that for our race tomorrow at noon, there will be few empty seats. If we're up there in the last 300m, the crowd will take us home. As we passed the stands today there were a few cheers for the home team. I can only imagine the madness to come.

Our Olympic heat went very well. We got out of the gate quickly, seized the lead and never looked back. We executed our moves almost flawlessly and finished more than two seconds ahead of the field. Our next stop was the Olympic final.

The U.S. Olympic eight looking strong en route to victory in our heat in the Olympic Games. (Photo courtesy of Joel Rogers)

Tuesday July 23, 1996   *Gainesville, GA*

Albeit a day late I got a super birthday present yesterday–a win in our preliminary heat and a trip straight to the Olympic final on Sunday. Yesterday was a crazy day, but thoroughly enjoyable. Just a taste of the excitement ahead if we can come through on Sunday.

After all the pageantry of the Olympic Games thus far, it was nice to put all that aside and strut our stuff a little. Considering the results of previous competition, yesterday's win was a much needed shot of confidence.

All of the sudden, I have goose bumps thinking about winning that race on Sunday. There are lots of similarities between '96 and '94–hometown fans, comfortable surroundings, long break between heat and finals, not being favored, and so on. The one similarity we need the most, the most elusive, is the chemistry. In '94, you could feel that we were on a mission. The nine of us were united in a common goal. We would overcome any obstacle to get that gold medal.

This year I am beginning to sense the resurgence of that magical feeling. The obstacles are just as tough–a Dutch eight no one has come close to, and the enormous pressure of the hometown fans. We have a bond amongst us. Each of us has to get in the boat and perform selflessly. We must row for the other eight. Only then we can win.

Friday July 26, 1996   *Gainesville, GA*

Time is rolling by. We have gotten through most of this interminable week of waiting already. Between playing pool, watching the regatta, satellite TV, and other distractions, the moment is now nearly at hand.

It seems like many pieces of the puzzle are coming together. We are building strong bonds amongst the crew, and we are focused on a single-minded drive towards victory. Plus, we are in the great role of the underdog.

The Dutch have won everything this year. I am not sure anyone has even led them at a 500m mark. Reportedly, one of their crew (seven man Ronald Florjin) told a reporter that they "expect to win by five seconds."

Let that overconfidence grow as far as I care. We have got eight of the toughest, fittest, most determined guys at this regatta. So far, we have gotten nothing in the way of respect. We floored the Germans in the heat, but everyone talks about the Dutch. All the better because of the way it sets us up psychologically. First, there isn't the pressure on us to win as home team favorites. Second, our lack of attention makes us all the more determined to prove everyone wrong.

Except for a slight bout of the nerves last night, I have been pretty relaxed. At our boat meeting we talked about the thirty-two year drought for the U.S. in the men's eight. Mike added that "the gold medal stays with you for the rest of your life... You don't get many opportunities."

Saturday July 27, 1996   *Gainesville, GA*

After three years of intense training, the final moment is at hand. Part of me can hardly believe that the Olympic final for the men's eight has arrived. Surprisingly, my nerves have calmed down a bit. Sure I feel a little tense, but I also feel as prepared as possible.

In the midst of all the excitement surrounding our competition tomorrow, I nearly forgot the story of the day. Upon arriving at the course, Spracky told us to be ready for increased security because of a bomb last night that killed a few people.

This minor fact certainly rattled each of us a bit. It even shook our concentration enough to make practice a bit worse. After the workout, news of the terrorist act was everywhere. Late last night around 1:30am, a pipe bomb exploded in Centennial Olympic Park. A 911 call was phoned in

moments earlier that alerted the bomb squad and diminished the potential number of injuries. Currently, there are two fatalities and over 100
injuries. Judging from the thousands who visit the park, it is amazing that
more people escaped serious harm.

This pathetic act has cast a dark shadow over the Olympic Games.
Personally, it made me more uneasy than just worrying about racing.
Now we have to worry about terrorism too? Unbelievable. I spoke to my
girlfriend this morning to make sure that everyone was okay. She confirmed that all of my family and friends were safe and sound. Time to get
re-focused on racing.

Sunday July 28, 1996   *Gainesville, GA*

8:50am
This is it. D-day. More than three years of training focused on today. I'm
pumped up to let it all hang out. We will leave for the course in seventy
minutes. Don, JB, and most guys are watching "Free Willy" for superstitious reasons–they saw it the morning of the final in Indianapolis.
Personally, I've got "Derek and the Dominos" jamming on CD and I am
trying to stay loose.

We have already been for a paddle this morning. By 7:30am, the stands
were starting to fill up. It should be a capacity crowd. Funny enough, the
weather is very mild, skies are overcast, and the forecast calls for light rain.
I guess all those hours in sweat suits in California and the heat chamber at
San Diego State went for naught.

Last night's final boat meeting was very emotional. It concluded by having
everyone make one last comment. Each of us was asked to dedicate the race
to someone. I told the guys how excited I was for that one opportunity
tomorrow. Then added that I had dedicated my race to them.

Lots of joking around this morning about how depressed we will all be when this is over. Jake said, "Yeah, so we better win to put off that depression." Funny, but true.

Only an hour left to hang loose before we leave. I am trying to block any thoughts of pressure out of my mind. I want to crank up my Discman with "Rage Against the Machine" and arrive at the course raring to go, ready to knock off anyone who stands in our way. We can be Olympic Champions. We're gonna get our shot at gold. Gotta let it all hang out.

I clearly remember the talk that Spracky gave the crew before we headed onto the water for the race. In almost all other pre-race talks, Spracky was loose, calm and even joking. This time his tone was very serious. At that point in the regatta, no American crew had won a gold medal. He asked us to do so. "This hasn't been a good regatta for America," he said. "Your country needs you now boys, your country needs you." His words sent a chill up my spine. I wanted to win for my country.

The Olympic final never developed as we had hoped. We had a strong pre-race warm-up and everyone seemed prepared for the challenge ahead. I've often thought back to the moments we sat on the starting line awaiting the official's call. I wonder if there is something I should have said or done that might have altered the ensuing race. As history would have it, we limped off the starting line and never challenged for the lead. At the finish line the order was Netherlands, Germany, Russia, Canada, USA and Australia.

The U.S. Olympic eight struggling toward the finish line in Atlanta.
Canada leads us by about seven seats and the Russian stern is just visible
on the right edge of the photo. The Netherlands and Germany are out of the
picture altogether. (Photo courtesy of Joel Rogers)

An ugly scene on the dock after the Olympic Final in Atlanta.
Instead of receiving our Olympic medals, we're trying to figure out what just
happened. (Photo courtesy of Joel Rogers)

Monday July 29, 1996   *Roswell, GA*

Fifth place.

It is all over. More than three years of intense emotional and physical commitment are done. As the sun rises this morning, I should feel a renewed sense of excitement, opportunity, and possibility. To tell the truth, I cannot feel a goddamned thing.

I had figured that I would be numb after the build-up to such a regatta. Every year I react differently, usually crawling into my shell somehow. But this year's result is the killer. Never in a million years did I think we'd finish fifth. Fifth. We were never really in the race from the start. We battled our way into medal contention through the middle, but spent too much doing it. In the end, we lost out on the final medal and fourth place too.

What a bizarre race. It seemed to be over in a flash. The start itself was particularly strange. First, they decided not to use the bonnets that hold the bows. There was a long pause between "Attention...Go!" that included some flinching amongst our crew. When we finally did get off the line, we were behind. It seemed like immediately Canada had three to four seats on us—a pretty big hole to dig out of.

Shocked by being down so much, I tried to convey a sense of urgency to the guys without going ballistic. We moved steadily, and even took over third place in the third 500m. In the sprint, the guys had already spent their pennies. Russia made a strong move and Canada squeaked by us too. When we crossed the line in fifth the only recognizable word was "Fuck." And it was said plenty.

After wallowing in our sorrow for a few minutes, we paddled the boat out of there and cruised home. Arriving on the dock, Mike was there to greet us. Expecting some mild form of sympathy, I was greatly mistaken. He came right up to me and asked, "What happened at the start? Why did you fall back so quickly? You were half a length down in the first ten."

I shook my head in disbelief. I was shocked at the recent results of the race, and also by his harsh line of questioning. The only answer I could muster was, "I know we fell back. I'm not sure why."

Next, we de-rigged the boat in silence, hurrying to beat an impending rain storm, and the arrival of the victorious Dutch. That would make us all sick. I kept my head for a while after the race. What killed me, though, was seeing Silken walk over with tears in her eyes to tell me she was sorry. That got my own faucets going.

We suffered through de-rigging, loading and other junk, then it was time to go into the real world. First stop, the media tent. I kept my head high, although my Oakley sunglasses hid my tear soaked eyes. I spoke with a number of reporters from **The Atlanta Journal-Constitution, USA Today,** *etc. It would be unprofessional to ignore them in defeat. A winner inside is not going to run and hide. Yet I had little to say. The race was still a shock. My best answer was about future plans—"To break three hours in a marathon and get my golf game in the 80's."[1]*

Next stop was potentially the hardest, my family. My parents especially seem to live and die through racing, and I thought they might be having a tougher time than me. All they can do is watch. Maybe that's why the pain is so great. Once I saw them, I resolved to lift their spirits, and those of everyone else that came to see the racing. If I could be "up," they would have to be.

I spent the rest of the afternoon visiting with more friends and family than I have seen in years. It was almost like an episode of "This Is Your

---

1   The day after our race the story in The Atlanta Journal-Constitution began: "Coxswain Steven Segaloff sat in a steady drizzle, his Olympic spirit left somewhere on Lake Lanier. Champagne corks popped all around, but no glasses were filled for him.
More than an hour before, he and the U.S. men's eight crossed the finish line fifth, in stunned silence. Oars splashed in the water in frustration. Heads shook. But no words were spoken.
"We're all in a state of shock," Segaloff said, slumped in his chair. "We've been going for this for four years and now it's over."

Life." Over fifty of my closest family and friends had gathered at my uncle's house in Atlanta. They had all made the journey to watch me compete in the Olympics. Until that afternoon I had seen no one. On the way there, I called to see how everyone was doing. When my sister Beth said, "Not too bad." I got a little fired up. I told her to give this message, "Tell everyone to pull their heads out of their asses and be happy. I can't deal with depression." I think it worked because it wasn't like going into a morgue.

The week following our competition in the Olympics was another roller-coaster ride. The Olympic Games continued for another week, but because our athletic responsibilities were finished, we were free to do whatever we wanted. The result was a week of wild times. By day, as Olympians, we had access to tickets for almost any competition. By night the city of Atlanta was on fire. Nights typically started out at a corporate function sponsored by companies like Sports Illustrated or Kodak, and then moved into Atlanta's club scene in Buckhead, where a flash of Olympic credentials was almost a sure-fire way to earn free drinks. On the whole, the week of partying was a chance to let out a lot of pent-up emotion. Despite all this fun, a part of me still mourned over our disappointing performance.

Friday August 2, 1996   *Olympic Village, GA*

What's troubling me most now is what I would call a "Patton complex." It is eating away inside me and tainting my every thought. I can only hope that time will ease some of the pain. I call it a "Patton complex" because the symptoms are very similar to those of my hero the late, great General.

Throughout his life Patton often wrote in his journal that he was destined for greatness. He truly believed that God meant for him to be a great leader of men. Despite a different set of objectives, I believe that I am destined for greatness. Coming into Atlanta I felt a huge wave of support. It was as if the stars were aligned for our crew. Right up until those precious moments on the starting line, I thought this was our time. I was sure that God had figured it all out. This race was my springboard to fame.

Five and three-quarters minutes later all those hopes and dreams were crushed. The master plan, of which I was so earlier confident, was erased. Our dismal fifth place finish not only dashed any hope of greatness, it ensured the label "mediocre" for our crew. In four years of world championship competition, fifth place is truly abysmal.

Where to now? Is my road to greatness closed? Or is this just an unexpected detour? How, where, and when do I begin anew down another road? What could possibly lie ahead?

Part of me refuses to let go of this Olympic dream. I had never really considered going beyond this season, but I never planned to finish fifth either. It is easy to think of staying with it since we're in the midst of the most rewarding two weeks, but four more years is a very long time. I am not sure that I could endure all that time with Spracky, especially with a boat full of new guys. That does not necessarily preclude my return in some later years as the 2000 Olympics get closer.

Forgetting the rowing for a second, I believe that the tragic lessons I have learned here in Atlanta could be the motivation I need for post-Olympic success. It is easy to get caught up in all this Olympic hoopla, but there is more to life. I gave my best and did not succeed. Life will go on. Now I need to pick myself up and start all over again.

How can I learn from what happened here? From today onward, I can take my destiny in my own hands. There is no more team to consider these days, just myself. I am free to determine my own success or failure on a purely individual basis.

Keeping that individuality in mind, I need to capitalize on my intensity and desire to succeed. For over three years, I have focused my energy on these Olympics. Now that they are over, I will have all the more ability to turn that attention to a newer, brighter dream.

The principles are the same—integrity, discipline, commitment, intensity, and desire; only the target changes. If I refuse to be denied, then life will work itself out.

Sunday August 4, 1996   *Olympic Village, GA*

Tonight is the Closing Ceremony of the 1996 Summer Olympic Games. I have much to reflect upon about the past sixteen days—ups and downs, tragedy and triumph. As I write today I still have many emotions left to discover. It is going to take some time to sort everything out.

Each day itself brings with it a wild array of feelings. Sometimes I feel so proud to a part of the U.S. Olympic Team. In other moments I find myself nearly in tears of grief.

One of the highlights of my post-Olympic experience was the team trip to the White House. The day after Closing Ceremonies, the U.S. Olympic Committee and the White House coordinated an amazing couple of days.

The morning after the Games officially concluded, several charter buses drove into the Olympic village to the buildings of the U.S. team. We packed up our bags, left them in the designated area, and boarded the charters. The buses drove to the Atlanta airport, onto the tarmac, and pulled up to the plane. Two separate planes carried the entire U.S. squad to D.C., where more charter buses met us immediately. A moment later, we were whisked to a hotel in McLean, Virginia where we were greeted by a few hundred cheering fans. In our rooms, we found our bags waiting for us. Travel was never so care-free.

We enjoyed more superstar treatment for two days in the Washington area. There were concerts, barbecues, and other parties. But the coolest part was definitely our morning at the White House.

The U.S. Olympic team spent half a day at the White House. Since the entire team gets to meet the first family, each athlete gets only about fifteen seconds of chat time with Bill, Hillary and Chelsea in a long receiving line. My handshake with the President was a bit of a letdown because it was so brief.

Just when I started to feel important enough to merit this treatment, I was brought right back down to earth. I ran into a thirteen year-old buzz saw named Dominique Moceanu. I spied the popular gymnast a few yards away on the White House lawn and decided to approach her for a picture. "Do you have a minute, Dominique?" I asked politely and held out my camera.

"Make it quick," the tiny mite tartly replied.

If I had any guts, I would have turned and walked away. But my lack of gumption forced me to stand there like a jerk and pose with the most self-important teenager I have ever met.

The Olympic eight enjoying the festivities at the White House.
Standing from left to right: Doug Burden, Bob Kaehler, Steven Segaloff,
Porter Collins, Ted Murphy, Jon Brown and Jamie Koven.
Kneeling from left to right Don Smith and Fred Honebein.

We had a few more days of star treatment after the White House, when Busch Gardens Williamsburg invited all Olympic athletes for an all-expenses paid vacation. After a few more days of lapping up the attention, it was finally time to head home. The odyssey was over.

As I rode the train back from D.C. to my home in New Haven I had just enough time by myself to become disappointed. I looked forward to some peace and quiet, and I looked forward to seeing family and friends. But I didn't look forward to heading home without an Olympic medal in my bag.

Chapter 5: Aftermath

What happened on July 28, 1996? Why did we lose? Why did we fail to live up to our previous expectations? Why did we fail to live up to our own expectations? Did all our mental and physical preparation fail? Did we over-train for the Olympics? Was our program too intense? Did we have the right people in the boat? Did we have the right race plan? Did we use the right boatmaker? What happened on July 28, 1996?

These are questions that I have contemplated almost every day since the Olympics. I wish there were definitive answers to any of these questions. I wish there was some way to justify the disaster on Lake Lanier that afternoon. If there is an answer I have not found it yet.

There are plenty of theories as to why we lost, and many of them may have some credibility. The bottom line, though, is that we failed to perform to our capabilities. After four years of training for one five and a half minute race, we failed to perform for those five and a half minutes.

The facts of the race clearly show our failure to perform. We gained a reputation as a fast starting crew from 1993 through 1995. We would crank out of the blocks and work hard to establish an early lead. The book on our crew internationally was that if you could stick with the Americans for the first half of the race, you could wear them down before the finish line.

On July 28th, we fell behind immediately. I recall looking out to the other crews in amazement at how far back we were so early. We found ourselves in a new and scary position. When you are used to being in the front of a pack at the start of a race and suddenly you are in the back, the results can be psychologically heart breaking. We tried to stick to our race plan and move through the field throughout the middle portion of the race. At one point, we even climbed into bronze medal position. But too much energy was spent in the grueling middle 1000m, and we had nothing left for the finish line. We had failed.

The fact that we had failed was obvious from those results, but the far more complex problem is WHY did we fail? There is no one answer to that question. Every critic has his or her favorite idea–over-training, wrong boat chemistry, wrong boat, wrong coach, wrong athletes or wrong line-up. There may be some validity to any theory, but I don't believe there was one major contributing factor. I believe that the way the 1996 season played out, we never really found our rhythm as a crew. We had too many ups and downs. One day we could perform at world-record pace, and the next day we would be as flat as an airless balloon.

In the end, I will defer to the harsh reality of sport. Races are run to definitively determine winners and losers. In my heart I believe that our 1996 Olympic crew was better than fifth best in the world. But on that given day, in that given race, that is what happened. And that is the reality we must embrace.

Saturday August 17, 1996   *New Haven, CT*

Every day I feel as if I'm standing on a precipice that separates me from reality and insanity. I still cannot believe that we choked away our golden opportunity. Three weeks ago tomorrow was the nightmare, and it still haunts me. I can only hope that the pain and anguish will subside in the weeks to come. Right now, it only seems to be getting worse.

The best I feel every day is at the end of a tough run. By pushing myself to a state of physical exhaustion I can relax my mind and ease the pure anger that courses through my veins otherwise.

It would be one thing if we had raced to the best of our abilities and came up short. Now I fear that I will live the rest of my life trying to figure out what happened on the starting line that made everything so wrong. Was it my fault? What could I have done differently to make it better? I wonder if I might have to jump back into the international rowing scene to exorcise the demons in my brain.

More than three full years of hard work and sacrifice–all so that we could finish fifth in the Olympics! Even as I write these words I pray that they are not true. Last week, I dreamt that we got another chance to race that final. After nearly an hour awake, I realized that my dream was just a dream. Again my heart sank to the ground.

Only after a few days of intense reflection can I begin to face the critics inside my head. What the hell happened on July 28th at noon? I remember sitting on the line below the overcast skies on Lake Lanier in Gainesville. I remember feeling totally at ease and ready to go. Perhaps I was too relaxed? I spoke calmly to the crew, and asked them to think about doing it "one time." Perhaps my tone was so relaxed that it failed to convey the attack mode we needed out of the gate? Perhaps, perhaps, perhaps. No matter how much second-guessing I do it will never change the results of the race. It is over and done with and nothing will bring it back.

The 1996 Head of the Charles was a fitting end to a bizarre and disappointing season. Since our eight had won the Championship Eight event in 1995, we kept our entry and our number one starting position for the next year's race. Although most guys from the Olympic team had quickly spread out around the country, many were still interested in racing in Boston. It is the annual rowing event that draws the most support in America, so many of us looked at this as a swan song opportunity. The Charles would provide one last weekend to get together, race for fun, and maybe even whip some people. I arrived in Boston a few days early to join the crew for training.

Sunday October 20, 1996   *Winchester, MA*

[12am] It is the night before the Head of the Charles, and I lay awake in my bed re-thinking the same thoughts that have plagued me for months now. My memories of that race still torment me nearly three full months after the Olympic final. I think back often to that fateful day, and now is as good a time as any to document the horrible visions flashing through my mind.

I remember how I felt sitting on that line, knowing that someone was about to be crowned Olympic champions, and hoping that someone would be us. I want to go back in time to that instant and relive the ensuing six minutes. I want to scream at myself to get the boat off the line faster in order to be up with the leaders. I want to go back and change our disastrous start. I want to go back and change everything.

Suddenly, the race has started, and I recall my view across–several seats down on the field. Not just a bad start, an awful start.

Gotta keep everyone cool. Don't freak out and get everyone in a tizzy. Try to stay levelheaded and get the boys back together. Damn, it's still not working. We're falling further behind. Gotta get going. Still, it's not time for urgency just yet.

We're through the middle of the race, and we're starting to get back into it. Maybe we can run out of here with a bronze medal after all. I hope so. Here comes the big commitment, now we're on the move. For a split second third place, bronze medal, something. Then it's gone.

The sprint has begun and we're falling off the pace. Damn, we're losing it. Gotta go faster, but it's not happening. With 250 to go a desperate cry from the middle of the boat, "C'mon! Let's go!" A new burst of power. Not together. Not effective. We're not going to do it.

Fifth place. It haunts me tonight. No medal. No bonus money. Nothing. Loser. The chance is over. My career is a disaster. It's done. The only sounds in the boat are repetitive curses every few seconds.

Unfortunately, the doubts have yet to go away. They plague me this week in Boston. They plague me tonight in bed. They follow me wherever I go. Am I a loser? I lost, didn't I? I let everyone down and choked in the big race. That's the final line in my script. Doesn't matter what happens tomorrow. Big disappointment. Fifth place.

[11am] In the thirty-five year plus history of the Head of the Charles, today is a first. The torrential rains and gusty winds have been so strong that the event was canceled. No race, no rowing, no nothing.

It seems only fitting that today was washed out. After the disappointment of this summer, my career may have just ended with one big fizzle instead of a bang. Rather than fighting things out on the water–and potentially winning a third straight Championship Eight title–this season ends with a cancellation. If this is the end of my rowing career, it truly is a wash.

The week after the Head of the Charles, another axe fell. Mike Spracklen was fired as head coach of the U.S. men's rowing team. I heard rumors around Boston that Mike was on thin ice. I did not want to believe it at the time, but was not very surprised when the word came out.

Mike is a strong personality, too strong to survive our inadequate performance in Atlanta. I would bet that people in power in USRowing were waiting in line to call Mike to tell him he was fired.

In order to deal with the depression after Atlanta I turned to another passion of mine in the ensuing months, marathon running. When I couldn't stand to think about the Olympics any more I laced up my running shoes and hit the road. I set my sights on the New York City Marathon and trained to break three hours.

Wednesday October 23, 1996   *New Haven, CT*

*In preparation for the upcoming New York City Marathon, I have been
putting myself through very intense training, including several two-hour
runs. If I am going to achieve my goal of a sub-three hour performance, I
need to complete a series of long training runs. One running friend encouraged me to complete three to four twenty mile runs in the month before the
actual race. That would definitely set me up nicely.*

*The point of this entry, though, isn't the training, but the pain. Often at
the end of a run, I yell at myself, sometimes audibly, "Come on, no pain.
No pain. Can't feel any pain." However, this exhortation is not what you
would think. I'm not trying to ignore the pain searing through my body in
those final moments. Instead, I feel as if the pain I have endured in the past
year significantly outweighs any physical pain of the moment. Specifically,
I'm talking about the pain of fifth place, the pain of selection, the pain of
trying to live up to a nation's expectations. Running with that kind of
anger, it's no wonder I have so much energy on the streets.*

Two weeks after the Head of the Charles I ran the New York City
Marathon. All of my months of training on the road were now focused
upon one race. Here was my chance to show that I could achieve a physical goal. I hoped to break three hours for 26.2 miles. I was determined
to succeed or feel enormous pain trying.

The scene at the start of the New York City Marathon is pure pandemonium. Approximately 30,000 runners squeeze through two levels of
the Verrazano Narrows Bridge on Staten Island. I arrived at the staging
area around 7am, nearly four hours before the starting gun, in order to
weasel my way to the front of the line. I was determined to get a fast start,
so I maneuvered into an ideal position. I was going to fly off the line.

Somewhere in the middle of the crowd was my teammate and buddy
JB. Jon is native New Yorker who promised himself that he would finish

this race someday. JB finished in four and a half hours and vowed that he would never run again.

My start was perfect, and I cranked out the first ten miles. Each one was considerably faster than I needed to break three hours. I reached the halfway mark in 1 hour 27 minutes and felt great. Somewhere around mile sixteen, though, I began to feel the pain of the sacrifice I had made in the first half of the race. I worried that I had gone out too hard. By the time I hit the twenty-mile mark, I was sure that I had gone out too hard. I began to pray for the race to end. My legs were heavier than cement, and I wasn't sure I could even finish. The winding, hilly miles through Central Park were tortuous. My mind and body were in upheaval. Only the presence of thousands of cheering spectators kept me motivated to press on. Breaking three hours was now a figment of my imagination. I only wanted to survive.

In the last mile of the marathon, the course leaves Central Park for a few blocks and then re-enters the park for the home stretch. On the final corner before re-entering the park, I hardly noticed my own cheering section. Mike Peterson, Jamie Koven, and a couple of other rowing buddies were standing on the corner cheering wildly for me. I was so disillusioned that I vaguely heard their raucous shouting when I was right next to them. For four seasons, I had watched those guys endure immense pain. In this final half-mile, the same guys delighted in seeing me in a similar death-like trance. That evening they treated me to dinner at an Italian restaurant. "Scrappy," Mike Peterson said, "Now you know how we feel. I would pay this bill every week to see you look like that again and again. It was great."

I crossed the finish line in 3 hours, 6 minutes and 10 seconds, a new personal best. I even managed to crack the top 1,000 runners by finishing 995th out of a field of more than 30,000. My mind was so blown away that I didn't know where I was. I walked through the finishing chute while a volunteer placed a medal around my neck and said, "Congratulations."

I looked her straight in the face and asked. "Am I done?"

"You sure are." she replied. "Now we're going to talk you to the medical tent."

For the next hour, I received treatment from the medical staff. I strained to walk under my own power, drank hot chocolate to keep warm in the chilly weather, and struggled to regain my sensibilities. I felt a sense of inner joy amidst these waves of pain. Only in physical misery could I forget about rowing and all the tragedies of the previous summer.

In time, the pain of our loss in Atlanta slowly diminished. I still thought about the race often, but I began to realize that there was more to life. Throughout the fall after the Olympics, I was invited to speak to a variety of groups–schools, synagogues, youth groups, and so on. Most speeches were given to children, which gave me the added value of knowing I had the opportunity to impart my "wisdom" to a wide-eyed audience. For half an hour, I was a winner again. I was no longer a fifth place finisher, I was an Olympian. More importantly, I had the chance to positively influence other people. I had a chance to make a difference. I looked forward to these talks as a kind of therapy.

The lesson of every speech I give is a variation on the theme of living life to the fullest. The point that I try to make is that you have to go after life with great enthusiasm. Whether it's rowing, writing, playing the violin, or another dream, you will never know how good you can be unless you give it everything you've got. You never want to look back upon a time in your life and wonder, "What if?" This was the same question that drove me back into rowing in 1993.

I embrace this credo because I know that the worst possible outcome is not reaching your goal. My teammates and I worked our butts off to get to the Olympics and try to win a gold medal. Not only did that not happen, but we came home empty-handed. The Olympics were the single biggest disappointment in my life. But time did not stop. My world did not come crashing down. Of course, I am painfully upset about what happened, and seldom a day goes by that I don't think about it. But no one goes through a career without experiencing loss at some time. That is sport–winning and losing. It is inevitable. The true champion is the one who can pick himself up and press on. Don't dwell on the past and wallow in your self-pity. Figure out what went wrong then work to make the next day a better one. In the end, you will still benefit by trying rather than sitting on the sidelines.

Despite the fact that I did not return from Atlanta with a medal, I have plenty to be proud of. I have three years of tremendous memories, innumerable new friends, a wealth of travel experiences, a drawer full of medals, honors, ribbons and much more that words cannot express. If I had not answered Mike Spracklen's phone call in 1993 I would have none of these things. I would not have this disappointment, but I would also not have the happy memories.

Since Atlanta I have developed this philosophy that sustains me today. There are still plenty of times when I look back upon the summer of 1996 with regret and sadness. But those sinking sensations of depression are typically overcome by a positive attitude. Regardless of how life's challenges arise in the future, I am determined to attack them with a positive attitude.

I have also realized another important lesson that I learned along my Olympic journey–PERSPECTIVE. When I watched the Los Angeles Olympics twelve years earlier I set my sights on Olympic glory. I pointed towards July 28, 1996 as the most important day in my life for four racing seasons. My teammates and I devoted everything in order to try to be the best in the world on that one day for five and a half minutes in time. Our entire lives revolved around that opportunity. We failed. The moment was gone, and our lives' focus was taken away. Once that race was over our sense of perspective was ruined. Wasn't the world going to stop spinning?

The lesson is that there is always another goal to strive for. Every athlete in the Olympics feels some sense of loss once their competition is over, win or lose. The glue that has held our lives together for years is gone.

Unfortunately, our crew's poor performance made the end of my competitive career that much harder.

It has taken me a long time to realize it, but the Olympics may not have been the biggest thing in my life. There are future opportunities for a career, a family, and other equally important events. I have reconciled the fact that I enjoyed an incredibly special time in my life–friends, travels, competition, and a small taste of glory. Now I have to move on, set other goals, and use the same determination and persistence to achieve them.

During the twelve years I competed in the sport of rowing, I came to know virtually every aspect of the sport. I coxed for men and women, young and old, beginners and elites, and winning and losing crews. I enjoyed the pinnacle of success as a world champion and the depths of depression in Olympic defeat. Along the way, I learned what it was like to have your ass kissed as a winner and your heart ripped out as a loser. Through it all I have tried to remain the same person. I have tried to maintain the same strength of character and integrity in the face of any situation. I may not have always been successful. In victory, it is hard to not think that you are better than others. In defeat, it is hard to get over the fact that you lost.

As the sign I saw every day prior to our world championship victory in Indianapolis proclaimed, "Success is a journey, not a destination." I believe that my twelve years of coxing got me started on that journey. Now, as I endeavor to tackle other challenges, I am confident that the lessons I learned through rowing have given me insight to make life's journey more fulfilling.

About the Author

Steven "Scrappy" Segaloff served as coxswain for the U.S. Eight-Man Crew from 1993 through 1996, including the 1996 Olympic Games. Mr. Segaloff grew up in New Haven, Connecticut. He is a graduate of Cornell University and a recent graduate of the University of Chicago Law School. Mr. Segaloff plans to practice law in New York City.